Twins, Triplets, and More

Twins, Triplets, and More

From Pre-Birth Through High School—
*What Every Parent Needs to Know
When Raising Two or More*

Elizabeth M. Bryan, M.D.

St. Martin's Press ❧ New York

Library of Congress Cataloging-in-Publication Data

Bryan, Elizabeth M.
    Twins, triplets, and more / Elizabeth Bryan.
        p.   cm.
    Includes index.
    ISBN 0-312-19533-8
    1. Twins.   2. Triplets.   3. Birth, Multiple.   4. Child rearing.
    I. Title.
    HQ777.35.B78   1992
    649´.144—dc20   92-1095
                                                            CIP

First published in Great Britain by Penguin Books

First U.S. Edition: June 1992
First St. Martin's Griffin Edition: January 1999

10 9 8 7 6 5 4 3 2 1

Contents

Acknowledgments

∙∙∙

THIS BOOK WAS made possible only through the help of several thousand twins (as well as triplets, quads, quints, and sextuplets) and their families, whom I have been privileged to meet since I began my work in this area in 1973.

My debts are too many and varied to adequately acknowledge but I would like to especially thank a number of people, whether twins, parents, or professionals, for their helpful comments on parts of the manuscript—Ilona Bendefy, Lizzie Holmes, Jo Jones, Frances Price, Sue Prior, Judith Richardson, Jeffrey Segal, Nancy Segal, Angela Taylor, Christine Tomkins, Susan Whitfield, and Joan Woodward. Responsibility for the contents of the book is, however, wholly my own.

Carol Heaton, my literary agent, not only had the idea for the book but encouraged me at every stage.

I dedicate this book to my husband, Ronald Higgins, in gratitude for his literary skills as well as for his loving support.

Introduction

∙∙

ONE COLD WINTER NIGHT in March 1973 I was woken by my bleep and called to the delivery ward of Hammersmith Hospital where I was the junior pediatrician "on call." Twins were being delivered by caesarean section under an epidural anesthetic. This meant that the mother was without pain but fully conscious. I do not know who was more surprised, she or I, as the babies emerged from the womb. One was a bouncing 6-pounder who looked as if he had had too much to drink; he was not only chubby but bright red. His brother, a little scrap of $3^1/_2$ pounds, was pale and wizened. Yet these two very dissimilar babies proved to be "identical" twins. Something very strange must have happened in the womb. I decided to discover more.

This quest marked the beginning not only of a two-year research project on the function of the placenta but of my preoccupation ever since with twins and their families, not to speak of triplets, quadruplets, and the even higher multiple births. A few minutes in a delivery ward had given birth to one pair of twins and my life's work.

My study of the placenta and the nourishment of the fetus in twin pregnancies involved regular visits to a hundred mothers and their twins until the babies were a year old. All the mothers were very helpful. I was not much help to them. All I could offer was a sympathetic ear and a means of contacting other parents of twins. I had been a children's doctor for some years but had known nothing about the special problems of caring for twins, and was astonished to discover how many there were. By the end of the year I was much less interested in the placenta than by what it was like to be a mother of twins or to be a twin oneself.

. . .

Since that time I have met many families with twins. I have never ceased to be fascinated by all the different facets of twinship which at once enrich and complicate the lives not only of the twins themselves but of all those concerned with them from the moment they are conceived—their parents, obstetricians, brothers and sisters, pediatricians, grandparents, friends, partners, and teachers.

Throughout this time I have been closely associated with the Twins and Multiple Births Association (TAMBA) which gives invaluable parent-to-parent support to families with twins, triplets, and more. I have been privileged to have close connections with it from its conception in 1978, when there were only twelve parents-of-twins clubs in the UK, until now when it acts as an umbrella for over two hundred clubs.

Much of my more recent experience has been gained from working in the Twins Clinics which were opened in London in 1987 and later in Birmingham and York. In 1988 the Multiple Births Foundation (MBF) was launched, which now runs these clinics and offers professional support to parents, and information and an education program to professionals. Many of the cases I have encountered in my work as pediatric consultant to TAMBA or as Director of the MBF have served as illustrations in this book. I have preserved confidentiality by changing names and distinguishing details. I have also tended to refer to the children as 'him,' mainly because it makes a clear distinction from the mother.

Everyone is interested in twins. Any mother who takes her babies out shopping will confirm that. Nevertheless, many people are also disconcerted or confused by meeting two people, whether children or adults, who are individuals yet indistinguishable from each other. Twins are attractions but also mystifying.

My long search for knowledge about twins has led me along many intriguing paths and I will try to share some of these with the reader. What kinds of twins are there? Why do they happen? What is it like to have two babies at once, to love two babies at once? Is the twin whose twin dies at birth still a twin? Why does the person whose twin dies later in life sometimes feel only half a person?

What happens when, perhaps due to a disability from birth, one twin has a very different mental and physical age from the other and yet looks very similar? How do twins react who have been separated at birth and then meet in adult life? What are the results of being born with two, three (or even five) brothers and sisters of the same age?

In pursuing questions like these I have found myself talking to parents of twins all over the UK, doctors in China, Japan, and Australia, nurses in South Korea, anthropologists from Nigeria, Caribbean health workers in Curaçao, and research workers at the famous twin centers in Minneapolis and Rome.

Foreword

∙∙

IT IS WITH GREAT PLEASURE that I invite the reader to savor this gem of a book. While the pleasures of raising twins and other higher-order births are great, the challenges are also formidable. Parents who have experienced the birth of multiples can benefit greatly from the proper material assistance, practical advice, and emotional and intellectual support. Dr. Elizabeth Bryan, a distinguished pediatrician, an invaluable friend, and professional consultant to the Twins and Multiple Births Association and the driving force behind the Multiple Births Foundation, has been providing such resources to families with twins and higher-order births for many years. *Twins, Triplets, and More* makes available, to the larger community of families of twins and higher-order births who do not have access to her or these valuable organizations, her extensive experience and accumulated wisdom. This book provides in clear, concise, and readable English the fundamental facts about the nature, development, and care of twins and higher-order births. It is the first book that anyone curious about twins and their care should turn to, and it is often the only source they will need. It is thorough. It is definitive. Every crucial question that a parent or potential caretaker of multiples is likely to ask is elucidated. Real and thoughtful examples inform every chapter. Dr. Bryan's clinical acumen, professional competence, breadth of scholarly knowledge, and caring and nurturant personality permeate every page.

You are in competent and caring hands. Enjoy.

Thomas J. Bouchard, Jr., Ph.D.
Professor and Director, Minnesota Center for Twin and
Adoption Research

Twins, Triplets, and More

The Biology of Twinning

THROUGHOUT HISTORY there have been all sorts of false and misleading ideas about twins and how they occur. The term "twins" is itself a very old one and is derived from the ancient German word *twina* or *twine* meaning "two together." In medieval times it was even thought that a boy and a girl could not share the womb together because it would be indecent—the *horror incestus!*

William Shakespeare was fascinated by twins and the confusion of identity to which they can give rise. In *The Comedy of Errors* he tells the tale of two masters, who appear to be identical twins, and gives each of them one of an identical pair as their servant. However, Shakespeare did not understand the difference between fraternal and identical twins. He was father to a boy and girl pair himself, Hamnet and Judith, and, like many early writers, he did not realize that male/female pairs could not be "identical" twins. In *Twelfth Night*, for example, we are told about Viola and her brother Sebastian that "an apple cleft in twain is not more twin than these two creatures."

But false ideas about twins are not just part of history. Even today many parents have quite unnecessary worries. Some farming people still believe that the female in a pair of twins of different sexes will be infertile in the same pattern as in cows, where the female grows up as a so-called "freemartin." But the placenta of a human mother is not like that of a cow and the hormones of the human male are not able to cross to the female, so cannot affect her fertility.

Several parents have told me they were worried that one or both of their identical twin girls would not be able to have children. It seems to be a quite widely held belief that identical twins are likely to be infertile, yet there are no grounds whatsoever for this fear.

What, then, are the basic facts about twins? What about the different types? How often do they happen? Why do they happen?

It has been known for centuries—albeit with no great clarity—that there are basically two different kinds of twins: identical twins who are very similar in looks and fraternal twins who look no more alike than any other brother or sister. It is only in our own century that the different origins of the two types have come to be understood.

We now know that identical twins are identical because they share the same genes. This means that they must have the same sex chromosomes too and thus the children will always be of the same sex. Identical twins arise when a normal fertilized ovum (egg) divides into two and each of the halves becomes a separate individual. Identical twins are therefore also known as uniovular (one egg), or monozygotic (one zygote—a zygote being a fertilized egg).

Identical twins will always not only be of the same sex but have the same basic physical features such as hair and eye color, although they may be of very different size and appearance if their nourishment has been different, whether in the womb or later.

There is, however, one rare condition in which identical twins are of a different sex. This is where one twin has the full complement of chromosomes including the XY sex chromosomes of a normal boy (or the XX of a normal girl) whereas the other twin has only forty-five chromosomes instead of forty-six. In such cases the Y or one of the X chromosomes is missing. This leaves a single X (female) chromosome and is known as Turner Syndrome. Such a twin develops as a girl even if the other twin is a boy. However, because she is missing her second X chromosome, she is not able to have children herself. She is also usually of rather short stature.

Fraternal twins occur when the mother produces two eggs instead of one in the normal monthly cycle and both of these are then fertilized. These twins are also known as nonidentical, binovular (two eggs), or dizygotic (two zygotes).

Although both fraternal twins will be conceived in the same

monthly cycle, the two conceptions may take place on different occasions as the woman remains fertile for several days during each cycle. This phenomenon is known as superfecundation and it is probably the explanation for the higher incidence of twins amongst couples who have frequent sexual intercourse.

In our monogamous society it is unlikely that the overall frequency of superfecundation will ever be known; when there is only one candidate for father we cannot usually know whether the babies were conceived at the same time or not. There have, however, been some well-established instances when it is clear that there are two fathers. This was first reported in 1810 when a white woman was known to have had intercourse with a white and a black man. It was obvious that each child had inherited his coloring from a different father.

There have since been a number of cases where double paternity has been plainly confirmed by blood testing, but very often such suspicions are unfounded. Mauriceau, a French obstetrician writing in the early eighteenth century, said, "another woman . . . likewise had two children—the one like her husband, and the other like the gallant. But this does not prove superfoetation* because sometimes different imaginations can cause the same effect."

If partners are of different race or if one or both partners are of mixed race, the pigmentation of their dizygotic twins may be very different, just as it may be amongst their other siblings. Unusually, with one white and one black parent the children may each appear to have inherited all the physical features of one parent, so that they appear to have completely different racial origins.

Superfetation (as opposed to superfecundation) is the term used to describe additional conceptions in later monthly cycles. If this occurs at all in man—which is doubtful—it is extremely rare.

There is increasing evidence that there may be a third type of twin, "half identical," so to speak. These twins would arise if an egg splits *before* being fertilized and each half is then fertilized by separate sperms. The genes inherited from the mother would be identical but those from the father would not. As yet we have no idea

---

*Presumably he meant superfecundation.

how often, if ever, this type of twin occurs. Nor does the possibility need to cause any difficulty for the twins or anxiety on the part of their parents.

The incidence of twins in the UK is currently about 1 in 75 pregnancies which means that about 1 in 37 children is born a twin. In 1996, 9,726 pairs of twins were born in the UK, 299 sets of triplets, and 11 sets of quads.

The figure for twin pregnancies that is often quoted is 1 in 80. This was true in the 1940s and 1950s but the incidence then fell steadily until in 1979 it fell to the lowest point of 1 in 104. Since then there has been a small increase each year and in 1989 the incidence was back up to 1 in 90. The fall was mirrored in other European countries and in Australia and the United States. Indeed, in the United States the decline started about ten years earlier.

We still do not know for certain why there was this fall in the incidence of twinning. A number of factors could have contributed. First, since the incidence of twins is related to frequency of sexual intercourse, a change in love-making patterns may have affected the figures. (Has television made such a difference?) More frequent sexual intercourse was probably the explanation for the sudden increase in twin births in the UK after the end of the Second World War and in the United States following the return of its troops from Vietnam. It has also been shown that twins are more likely to be conceived in the first few months after marriage. This too may be due to a higher frequency of intercourse.

Second, the number and potency of the man's sperms affects the chances of an egg (or more) being fertilized and American research workers have suggested that these may have been reduced by some of the toxic substances now present in the environment and in our diet.

Third, women are having smaller families and are completing them at a younger age: the significance of this will be discussed later.

All these factors may have contributed to the decrease in the incidence of twins, but even taken together they do not seem to be an adequate explanation. And now the incidence of multiple births is rising again. Some of this rise, certainly that of triplets, can be explained by the increasing use of various forms of infertility treatment. We do not, however, yet know what other factors are involved in a somewhat complex overall picture.

Changes in twinning rates are due largely to changes in the incidence of fraternal as opposed to identical twins. It seems that the incidence of identical twins remains remarkably steady both over time and throughout the world at three to four pairs per thousand, although recently there has been a small—and unexplained—increase. Fraternal twinning rates, as we shall see, vary greatly between different ethnic groups.

The "incidence" of twins refers to the number of pairs of twin babies per thousand *completed* pregnancies. It does not indicate the number of twins conceived nor does it take account of those who die in the womb before the pregnancy has reached twenty-four weeks. Many more twins are actually conceived than are ever born. Only since ultrasound scanning became a routine part of prenatal care has it been realized that a large proportion— perhaps over three-quarters—of pregnancies that start with twins end up with only one baby.

When this happens, one of the babies usually dies very early in the pregnancy, before the twelfth week, and is reabsorbed into the placenta. This is known as the vanishing twin syndrome. Before the arrival of ultrasound scanning most of these mothers never even knew they had conceived twins.

There are a number of twin pregnancies, though a much smaller proportion, where one baby may die after the twelfth week but before the twenty-fourth week of the pregnancy. Such a baby is not reabsorbed but it will, of course, stop growing and then gradually shrivel up. At birth the parchment-like baby remains and this is known as *fetus papyraceus*—a "paper fetus." At present these twins, like miscarriages, are not recorded in the birth figures.

As in any pregnancy, there is a roughly 50 percent chance of each conception being a girl or a boy. Thus half of all fraternal twin pairs will be boy/girl pairs, a quarter will be two boys, and a quarter two girls. As almost all identical twins must be of the same sex (except in the very rare occurrence of Turner Syndrome), it is possible to calculate the proportion of identical and fraternal twins in a given population and this calculation is known as Weinberg's differential method.

In the UK approximately a third of twins are identical and two thirds fraternal. This means that a third of all twins will be boy/girl, one third both boys, and one third both girls.

Why do twins happen? The popular explanations for twinning given in different parts of the world owe much more to imagination than to science. In South Korea I was told that if I ate a double banana I would have twins. In Malaysia I heard that a double chestnut or millet seed would have the same effect. Some South American Indians are said to believe that if a mother lies on her back during labor the baby will split in two.

Nearer home, a tumbler full of water from the spring at St. Mungo apparently resulted in twins for the medieval Scottish. Shock has also been blamed for multiple births. A contemporary account of an earthquake in Hereford in 1661 reported that the shock had caused a clerk's wife, Mary Pelmore, to have triplets (all boys and boys moreover who had teeth and spoke as soon as they were born!).

We may realize that ideas of this kind are absurd but so far as identical twins are concerned, we actually have no more idea of the causes than the most remote Korean villager. It appears that all women who can conceive have the same chance of having identical twins. The only exception to this are very rare couples where one partner appears to have a dominant gene for identical twinning running through their family. Anyone would know if they belonged to one of these rare families as family gatherings would inevitably lead to rather more than the usual confusion.

Even with fraternal twinning we can never say to a woman, "If you become pregnant you will have twins," but we can at least say who is most at risk. Having looked at all the known predisposing factors it seems that if you are longing to have twins it is best to be a 6-foot Nigerian in your late thirties who already has five children including a set of fraternal twins. If the last thing you want is twins, it is best to be Japanese, 4 foot 11 inches, aged 20, having your first pregnancy, with no history of twins in the family.

Race strongly affects the chances of having twins. Black races, and particularly, it seems, Nigerians, have the highest rates of twinning. The Asian (or "Mongolian') races have the lowest rates. Caucasians and Indians are somewhere in between. The incidence of twins is about five times higher in the Yoruba people of Nigeria than amongst the English and ten times higher than amongst the Japanese.

Studies have shown that the level of the hormone gonadotrophin is higher in Nigerian women than in Japanese, and those Nigerian mothers who have twins have even higher levels. Gonadotrophin is a hormone produced by the pituitary gland which stimulates the ovaries to mature and release their eggs into the fallopian tube. If high levels of gonadotrophins are present in the blood a second (or more) egg is more likely to be released.

In racially mixed partnerships it is only the mother's race that has an effect. The rate of twinning in urban Africans is lower than those living in the country. Diet may be an important factor, and the yam has been suggested as the culprit for rural Africans; the hormone-like substances it contains may have an effect on the mother's fertility.

The chance of a mother of any race delivering twins increases until her late thirties. Parity also has an effect: the more children she already has, the higher her chances of twins.

It is widely believed that twins run in families and this is true, as I have said, of fraternal but not of identical twins. However, much confusing folklore accumulates round this basic perception like the often quoted notion that twins skip a generation. There is little to support this idea. The chances of having twins are increased, probably about fivefold, for a woman who is herself a *fraternal* twin or has fraternal twin siblings or has already had fraternal twin children. This means that she has more than a one in twenty chance of having twins in any particular pregnancy. Indeed, any fraternal twin relatives on her own side of the family increase her chances.

There are many families who have had a second set of twins and a few with three. The current world record for multiple births is held by Leontina Albina from Chile who had her 55th child in 1981. Her 55 children included 5 sets of triplets. The historical record is claimed for a Russian who is said to have had 69 children in 27 confinements including 16 pairs of twins, 7 sets of triplets, and 4 sets of quads. This would have meant that she had no singletons at all. She died in 1782.

Whether the father has any influence on the production of twins has been heatedly debated for several decades. Fathers themselves, naturally, wish to take some credit for the achievement! The majority of studies, however, suggest that the father's genes have little, if any, effect on the chances.

Currently the strongest single influence affecting a mother's chances of producing twins will be the use of infertility treatments such as ovulation stimulating drugs or the new techniques like *in vitro* fertilization (IVF) and gamete intrafallopian transfer (GIFT). These will be discussed in chapter 13.

Apart from asking whether the twins are all right, the first question parents most often ask about their new babies is whether they are identical or not. The parents may later be driven to distraction by this same question being asked by every friend and even casual passersby. For this reason alone parents want to know the zygosity (identical or fraternal—monoygotic or dizygotic) of their twins as soon as possible, but there are other good reasons for getting this clear.

It is only natural for parents to want to learn all they can about their babies; and later, the twins themselves are usually keen to know. Zygosity does, of course, affect the chance of a girl twin having twins herself, in the same way as it will affect the mother's chance of having another set. Thus the knowledge may affect a couple's decision as to whether or when to have another pregnancy. Furthermore, if either twin has some hereditary disorder the chances of the other twin being affected will depend on the zygosity.

If, later on, twins are prepared to be involved with any twin studies, then knowledge of their zygosity would again be crucial.

So how can zygosity be determined? In a third of the cases it is straightforward because the babies are of different sex and so must be fraternal (except in the very rare instances of Turner Syndrome—see p. 2). In most of the other cases it will become clearly apparent by the time the children are 2 or 3 years old, but many parents do not want to wait so long. Moreover, there are always some borderline cases in which it is difficult to tell.

First, we can look at the placenta. There are two main types of placenta in twin pregnancies. The first is a single placenta with a single membrane, the chorion: this is a single chorion or monochorionic placenta. The chorion is attached to the placenta and encloses the two babies like a sac. Within the chorion there are usually two inner sacs made from the thinner membrane, the amnion. Each baby has its own amniotic sac and is therefore separated from its twin. Occasionally, there is only one amniotic sac and the babies are then swimming together in the same sac, a monoamniotic as well as monochorionic placenta. If the placenta is monochorionic the babies *must* be identical. This is the situation in two-thirds of identical twins.

If, however, the egg splits very early, within the first five days or so of fertilization, the placenta will not have begun to form and separate placentas therefore develop, each with their own chorion and amnion. This dichorionic placenta is the second type of placenta and is found in a third of identical twins as well as in all fraternal twins.

Sometimes in both fraternal and identical twins the two placentas fuse together as they grow. Whether this fusion occurs will depend on where the tiny embryos have implanted themselves in the wall of the womb. If one is at the front and the other at the back, they will clearly never fuse. If they are side by side, they may well do so but the two chorions will remain forming a thick dividing membrane, made up of two chorions and two amnions, between the two babies.

In the case of like-sex twins with two chorions, the next test to be done is a blood test either for blood groupings or DNA "fingerprints." Because they have the same genes, identical twins will have the same blood groups whereas fraternal twins will have some similar blood groups and some different ones. Blood tests are most easily done by taking blood from the two umbilical cords attached to the placenta, although the blood can be taken at any age from the children themselves. If enough different blood groups are measured and found to be the same, the chances of the babies being identical are well over 90 percent. Considering the benefit involved it is unfortunate how few hospitals carry out routine determination of zygosity. The service is usually limited to centers undertaking twin studies, where knowledge of zygosity is essential.

The most accurate method of all is by DNA microprobe technique (as used for identifying criminals from blood or other body fluids). Unfortunately this is an expensive test. However, the advantage of DNA testing is that it can be done painlessly on samples of saliva or swabs of the membrane lining the mouth (a cheek swab) as well as on blood and the placenta.

Twins have long been a source of fascination but gemellology, the scientific study of twins, has emerged only in the last two centuries. Two people in particular have been responsible for promoting the study of twins.

The first was Sir Francis Galton (1822–1911) who realized that twins could be invaluable in the study of the effects of heredity and environment on human development. His classic *The History of Twins as a Criterion of the Relative Powers of Nature and Nurture* was published in 1876.

The second was Professor Luigi Gedda, from Rome, who is still actively working for twins, their families, and those who study them. As Professor of Medical Genetics at Rome University he founded the Instituto di Genetica Medica e Gemellogia and in 1951 wrote a review of all aspects of twins (*Studio dei Gemelli*) which was later translated into English in 1961 as *Twins in History and Science*.* In 1974 he became the founder president of the International Society for Twin Studies which has become the leading international organization for the promotion of research on all aspects of twins and higher-order births. Geneticists, pediatricians, psychiatrists, obstetricians, epidemiologists, psychologists, as well as parents and twins themselves, are amongst the members. The Society holds an international congress every third year and publishes its own journal, *Twin Research*.

_____

*C. C. Thomas (Illinois), 1961.

Multiple Pregnancy

I VIVIDLY REMEMBER the look of astonishment on the face of a father who was in the delivery room proudly admiring his baby daughter, now five minutes old, and for whom he and his wife had been waiting for eight long years, when the midwife, who was trying to deliver the placenta, suddenly said, "There's another." And out popped a bouncing 5-pound son.

Until about ten years ago it was not unusual for the second baby to be discovered only after the delivery of the first. Since the introduction of routine ultrasound scanning in pregnancy this is now rare and only very occasionally happens if one baby is somehow hidden behind his twin. Similarly with triplets or more, one baby may occasionally be "lost." One mother who already had one child of two was told at her first scan she was expecting twins. Four weeks later a second scan showed triplets. When she finally delivered the babies a small but healthy fourth baby was found who had been hiding in the back of the womb.

Clearly it is much better that parents should have good warning of two babies. This is not only true from the practical viewpoint of getting prepared (and enrolling a bigger army of knitters), but also emotionally. It is nearly always a shock—however pleasant—to hear you are having twins. It is better to get over the shock well before the babies arrive.

For mothers who discover twins late in their pregnancy it can be quite disconcerting to find that the baby they have already come to love is, in fact, two. Which of these babies were they relating to? Or was it half of each? A mother who had only heard she was having twins when she was thirty-three weeks through her pregnancy, told me that the sensation of discovering a second baby was "quite eerie." A sad example of the emotional confusion is given by a mother who did not know she was carrying twins until the second baby was born. This second baby died soon after birth. The mother's distress was compounded by her uncertainty as to whether she had lost the baby she had been loving for so many weeks or whether the baby that had died had been unknown and therefore deprived of the love she felt it deserved. Some people would regard such confused and confusing feelings as irrational. I believe they are very powerful and important and must be treated with respect by parents, relatives and friends, and by the medical professionals as well.

Ultrasound has, however, brought with it its own problems. "I thought it must be a monster," one mother said to me when she first realized that the staff were seeing something different about her ultrasound scan. Many mothers who later have twins have a time of intense anxiety before they realize that the twins are the reason for the perplexed or concentrated look on the face of the ultrasound operator. The suspense is rendered far worse if a second opinion is needed, especially if this is not available until the next day. Medical staff need to be highly sensitive in these circumstances and reduce anxieties as much as possible even when they cannot give a definitive interpretation.

A second dilemma is when to tell the parents about a twin pregnancy. As discussed in the previous chapter, we now know that many mothers who conceive twins go on to deliver a single baby. In the old days neither the parents nor the doctor would ever have known about the second baby's existence. Many people therefore ask whether there is any point in risking upsetting the parents by giving them hopes of twins, only to shatter them a few weeks later when a second scan shows that one of the babies has disappeared.

I believe that a mother has the right to know. It is her body, and they are her babies. Also the fact that she has conceived twins means that her chances of doing so again are greater than average, so she might appreciate the warning.

Sometimes twins have already been suspected before the first ultrasound scan. The mother may be much larger for her dates than she would expect, or perhaps she is feeling different from previous pregnancies—some mothers suffer more sickness. Some have the worry of an abnormally high level of alphafetoprotein in their blood; a test for this is done routinely to check for spina bifida in the babies. What the doctor too often forgets to tell a mother is that a high level may be due to the presence of two babies. (The protein being tested for is produced by the baby.)

The news of twins nearly always seems to come as a shock. It was so even to a mother I knew who had nine known sets in her family! People just don't seem to believe it can happen to them. For some, of course, it is a happy shock. For others, particularly if the pregnancy was unplanned or finances are strained, it is a horrific one. For most parents it is a mixture. On the one hand they worry about how they will cope, financially and practically (not enough hands, small house or car etc.). On the other hand they are excited at the idea of having two babies, of watching two children exploring and enjoying life together. And most parents take pleasure in the attention, sometimes even celebrity treatment, they suddenly start to receive from friends and obstetricians alike.

To help a couple recover from the shock and to give knowledgeable reassurance, there are none better than parents who have been through it themselves. Few doctors or other medical staff have much relevant experience to offer. Parents of twins can answer the flood of questions that are bound to arise. As soon as a mother is told she is expecting twins she should be put in touch with others who have been through it all. In many countries there are local parents of twins clubs, most of which will come under the umbrella of a national organization, which can provide literature and general information as well as hold conferences.

This is not the book in which to describe a twin pregnancy in detail. It may, however, be helpful to look a little at the ways in which a twin pregnancy may be different from a single one. The most obvious difference is that everyone is much more interested in it. Friends and family are intrigued by twins and always regale expectant parents with every story they have heard on the subject, often misleading ones.

Many parents come to special MBF prenatal meetings for those expecting twins with all sorts of unnecessary anxieties. Some expect to have to go through the whole of labor a second time after the first baby has been born. Some fear the delivery will be much harder or that they might necessarily need a caesarean section. Many want to talk about epidural anesthetics. Others have been told that the babies are bound to be small. (In general, twin babies do grow more slowly than singletons during the last third of the pregnancy, but in the important early stages they grow just as well.) They have also often been told that twins are likely to stay smaller and slower than other children—which is just not true.

A twin pregnancy tends to be more tiring than a single one mainly because of the extra weight that has to be carried. After all, by thirty weeks a mother with twins is often the size of a mother of a single baby at full term. Much more rest is therefore needed and some obstetricians recommend a stay in the hospital for this. Other obstetricians will just recommend extra rest at home and instead keep a close eye on the mother as an outpatient, watching particularly for early signs of complications, such as preeclamptic toxemia with high blood pressure, so that these can be treated immediately.

In the old days there used to be worries about the second twin suffering from lack of oxygen to the brain while awaiting delivery. With modern technology the condition of the second baby can be carefully monitored and today the second baby seems to be at no greater risk than the first. The only advantage of being born first is when an inheritance is at stake in one of the countries where it always goes to the first-born. There are parts of the world, however, where it is an advantage to be the second-born. In parts of Nigeria the first-born is considered to be the younger twin as he is sent by the elder (and stronger) to see if the world is ready to receive his senior brother.

Birth order has held a greater significance in history and

mythology. We hear of the struggle in the womb between Jacob and Esau as to who should be born first, and also between Pharez and Zarah, grandchildren of Jacob. Amongst the Zulu tribes only the first-born was named. In many Indian stories the first-born is the hero and the second-born, the villian. In some African tribes and amongst some American Indians the second-born twin used to be smothered at birth. In others, both twins were killed. In many of the world's peoples, from the Eskimos of the American North to Australian aborigines, from the Ainu of Japan to the Indians of South America, there has been a deeply held fear and dislike of twins. There are several theories as to why this should be so. These include the idea that the second twin was conceived by an evil spirit or at least through an act of adultery. Others say that it is animal-like to have more than one baby at once. But the prejudices may well have arisen at least in part as a response to circumstance, the physical and economic burden of having two babies, particularly for nomads, when breast-feeding two babies would pose quite a challenge.

Antipathies arose in some tribes in relation to boy/girl pairs. Incest in the womb was suspected and for this reason some would kill the babies. Other peoples such as the Bantu and some Japanese expected these babies to marry later as they had been "married in the womb."

Because twins are more likely to be lying in unusual positions when labor starts, caesarean sections are more common with them than with singleton babies. Even so, the majority of twins are delivered by the normal vaginal route. Occasionally, if the second baby is in an awkward position, he will be delivered by caesarean section after the first has been delivered vaginally. In about half of twin pregnancies at least one baby will present breech (bottom) first, compared with only 3 percent of singleton pregnancies, and in nearly 10 percent both present by the breech. Delivering a baby by the breech tends to be more difficult than by the head.

Twin pregnancies can, however, have their compensations. Some mothers have told me that the labor and delivery of their twins was less difficult than that of a previous single child. This is probably because the babies were smaller and therefore easier to deliver.

Most second babies follow quickly after the first, within twenty minutes or so. It used to be thought unwise to wait longer, but there is not the same rush now that the second twin can be monitored while still in the womb. The delivery can always be hurried on if the baby shows signs of becoming distressed. There are many stories from earlier days, and still currently from some developing countries, of extraordinarily long intervals between the births of the two babies. The record was a twin who followed three and a half months after his brother. I had to reassure a mother that a long delay did not mean she would have to stay in labor for all that time! Occasionally nowadays we actually try to postpone the delivery of the second twin; for instance if one baby is born very prematurely it would obviously be better for the second to wait to grow and become more mature before being born. One report described twins where one baby was born weighing 14 ounces and died because he was so premature. The other was born sixty-five days later weighing over 3 pounds and survived as a healthy child.

A twin pregnancy can often *feel* longer than a single one because the mother, as well as other people, tend to be conscious of the pregnancy earlier. Furthermore, the restrictions of activity that occur toward the end of any pregnancy start much earlier with twins. In fact, the average length of a twin pregnancy is about thirty-seven weeks, three weeks *shorter* than the average singleton pregnancy. Identical twins tend to deliver slightly earlier than fraternal twins.

What triggers the onset of labor is uncertain. The size and therefore the distension of the womb cannot be the only explanation. Were it so, the average length of pregnancy would be when the combined weight of the two babies was about 7 pounds, whereas the average combined weight of twins is about 11 pounds. It may be that a combination of factors is responsible for starting labor; the high hormone levels in the mother's blood may well be one of these. Twins are more common amongst older mothers, as is the occurrence of such birth defects as Down's syndrome and spina bifida. If a woman is planning to be tested for such an abnormality it is technically possible to test the two fetuses (or even more) separately. This can be done either by chorion villous sampling (a tiny piece of the developing placenta is examined during the first ten weeks), or later by amniocentesis (when the amniotic fluid surrounding the baby is examined).

If both babies are normal, the parents can feel reassured. If both are abnormal, it is a tragedy but a decision to terminate the pregnancy is probably no more complicated than with a single child. Indeed, many might feel the decision to terminate would be even easier in that the care of *two* children with very special needs could possibly be viewed as an unbearable task. In these circumstances most couples who had actually chosen to have the test done would then proceed to have the pregnancy terminated.

If one baby is normal and the other abnormal the dilemma can obviously be agonizing. In the past the choice lay between terminating the pregnancy and sacrificing the normal child or continuing the pregnancy in the knowledge that one baby would be handicapped and require special care from the parents at the same time as they were responding to the needs of a healthy child.

There is now however, another choice, that of selective fetocide. The abnormal fetus can be killed in the womb and the pregnancy then continues normally for the other baby. Unfortunately it is not possible to remove the dead baby because the operation might make the mother go into labor and miscarry the whole pregnancy. It therefore stays in the womb and becomes a *fetus papyraceus* (see p. 5). For many couples selective fetocide may be the least painful of the options facing them, but they will still need a lot of support. They will lose a very precious baby and they may not feel the full impact of this loss until after the healthy baby is born. It may not be until then that the mother really acknowledges to herself that she is not, after all, a mother of twins. Conjoined (or Siamese) twins are always identical twins. In order to produce two healthy, normal identical twins the fertilized egg must split completely. If the egg does not split until about the fourteenth day after fertilization the division may not be complete and this is how conjoined twins are believed to be formed.

Conjoined twins can be connected at any point of their bodies but any given pair will be connected at the same point whether chest, abdomen, head, etc. The extent to which organs or limbs are shared, however, varies. For instance, Masha and Dasha, a pair of Russian twins now approaching their forties, share a single lower half to their body but are entirely separate from the waist upward. Other pairs are only connected by a small area. Chang and Eng, the "original" twins from Thailand, then called Siam, were linked only by a fibrous band between their chests which nowadays could easily be divided without injury to either baby.

Although conjoined twins always partly share a blood circulation (even if only connected by a small piece of tissue), some of their body functions may be quite independent. For instance, heart rhythms may differ and if one woman partner becomes pregnant the other may continue to menstruate.

Producing such twins is, of course, very distressing but they are very rare, perhaps one in every 50,000 to 100,000 pregnancies (the majority are female twins). Recently many pairs have been successfully separated and certainly this would always be attempted where possible. However, there are pairs where, because they are sharing vital organs such as a heart, the babies cannot be separated and some have gone on to live happy and productive lives. One nineteenth-century pair, Millie and Christine from North Carolina, were singers—Millie was the contralto and Christine the soprano.

Indeed, Chang and Eng, who were born in 1811, led active lives to the extent that they married two American sisters and one had ten children and the other twelve. They apparently ran two family homes, spending a few days in one before changing to the other. As with other identical twins, conjoined twins may have very different personalities and tastes. Sometimes this can be very hard on one or the other of the twins. When Chang took to drink Eng had to share the hangovers as the twins shared their blood circulation.

Masha and Dasha have had to learn to accept their differences, not least their different personalities. Dasha is the spokeswoman, whereas Masha is quieter and more easily upset. This intelligent pair spent much of their childhood disagreeing, even fighting. If one wanted to read and the other to go for a walk there was often a long argument. Masha likes to watch sport on television and Dasha prefers the chat shows. Masha would like to swim but Dasha is frightened of water. Now they have learned to compromise and take turns over the choice of activities.

Much has been said of the idea that identical twins may be mirror images of each other, that is, if the features on one twin are reversed then the mirror image thus created will be most similar to the appearance of the second twin. In such cases one twin may be left-handed and the other right, and some physical features such as fingerprint patterns, hair whorls, and dental patterns may be reversed. Less commonly, internal organs such as the heart or liver may also be reversed. Mirror-imaging, which rarely causes any problems, has been said to occur in up to 25 percent of identical twins and about the same proportion are opposite-handed.

The explanation that used to be given for mirror-imaging was that the division of the fertilized egg took place after the left and right sides of the developing embryo's body had been designated. This now seems an unlikely explanation, as when the egg splits the embryo is still a mass of undifferentiated cells. However, no more likely explanation has yet been put forward.

Most studies have found that twins have a higher incidence of left-handedness than single children but the proportions reported vary enormously.

3

Newborn Twins

··

Few of us expect to fall in love with two people at the same time. Indeed, it would be very awkward if we did. Yet this is precisely the challenge that faces the parents of twins. Many find it much more difficult than they expect. They often assume it will be easy and "natural" to love one's babies whether just one or more. This is not always so. In what follows I write mainly about the mother's responses but most of it applies equally to the father's responses which are, of course, vitally important in the development of the twins, and indeed of the whole family. A later section is devoted to fatherhood (see chapter 4), but fathers must forgive me meanwhile if, for the sake of brevity, I do not constantly refer to them.

Before the babies are born most mothers expect and plan to love their babies equally. When they arrive, however, it may be a very different story. For a start, one baby may be more immediately lovable than the other or may have a temperament that fits more easily with that of the mother. This was clearly shown in one of the families I knew in my original study.

Jane's first-born baby, Helena, weighed 7 pounds at birth and was an attractive, contented baby who fed well from the start. When she was put down she did not complain but always enjoyed a cuddle when it was offered. Helena's twin, Susan, was quite different. She had obviously received a poor share of nourishment in the womb. She was a pale, scraggy baby weighing only 4 pounds, and was unhappy and irritable. When her mother tried to comfort her she went stiff in her arms. She struggled if put to the breast and feedings took a frustratingly long time. No amount of cuddling seemed to comfort her but she cried even more when put down. Inevitably her mother had to spend much more time with her than with Helena. She began to resent Susan who was giving her no pleasure and, furthermore, depriving her of precious time with Helena.

Sometimes the difference in the mother's response may be due to an instant and seemingly superficial dislike or attraction. Another mother had never liked red hair. When she saw that one of her babies had a beautiful crop of thick black hair and the other some rather thin strands of ginger, she was immediately more attracted to the first baby. In this case, however, the feeling passed after only a few days when she got to know the ginger-head as a person.

The problem of relating to two babies at once is increased for the parents if they have difficulty telling them apart. If the mother has to unwrap the baby and scrutinize the little band round the baby's wrist before knowing if it is "Twin 1" or "Twin 2" and therefore Ben or Tom, before even starting to relate to the baby, she is wasting precious relating time. It is essential that the babies are made readily distinguishable right from the start—different color crib covers, or different toys, mean that the parents can start relating to each baby even before they reach the crib.

Relating to a baby can also be difficult for a mother when she is not able to nurse the baby. Clare's babies were very premature, born twelve weeks early. Sam, the first-born, weighed nearly 3 pounds and did remarkably well. After a few days of extra oxygen to help him breathe, he made excellent progress. His mother was allowed to handle him and helped with his care right from the start. Fiona, however, weighed only just over 2 pounds. She was extremely ill for many weeks. Her mother was terrified she was going to die; she tried not to think about it and just spent more time with Sam.

Even had she wanted to, she could not hold Fiona because of all the wires which attached the tiny baby to the machinery monitoring her breathing, her heart rate, her blood pressure, her temperature, her oxygen level, and so on, and all the tubes that helped her to breathe and to give her food.

After six weeks Sam was ready to go home. Clare was thrilled and put all her attention and energy into loving and looking after her son; she really did not want or need another child. She lived a long way from the hospital and did not have a car. Visits to Fiona were a major undertaking and when Clare did get to the hospital she just felt guilty that she could find no love for her daughter.

When Fiona finally came home she was not an easy baby. She cried a lot and took a long time to feed. Life became exhausting for Clare. She did have some help from the social services but this just made her feel even more guilty, and she also resented the loss of her privacy. Clare thought of Fiona as an intruder and resented the time she had to spend with her which could have otherwise been spent enjoying Sam.

It was many months before Clare came to love her daughter but, thanks to some continuing support and her own determination, she did in the end manage it and forged a happy relationship with her.

Some stories end less happily, particularly if the mother does not have enough understanding and support at the beginning. She may then never relate happily to the second child. Occasionally that child may have to be formally taken into care and even put up for adoption.

Fortunately, now that more support and understanding are given to parents with premature twins, most have overcome any initial feelings of strongly preferring (or rejecting) one of the twins by the time the babies are ready to go home.

It is fascinating to see how early twins show their different personalities. Mothers will often describe the differences immediately apparent in their babies' behavior and cries in the maternity hospital. This is less surprising with fraternal twins but is true even with identical twins, and suggests that experiences in the womb may have a profound effect.

Through ultrasound scans we are now learning much more

about babies' activities before they are born. In the case of twins, their relationship with each other as well as their individual activities can be demonstrated. Some babies appear to relate harmoniously, touching and stroking each other, whereas others seem to be having a constant battle. Often one baby is much more active than the other. Preliminary studies have shown that the babies continue to show these patterns of behavior during infancy.

The naming of their babies is an important task for all parents: with twins, the sooner it can be done the better so that friends and medical staff, as well as the parents, can refer to the babies as individuals right from the start. There is a great temptation to label babies as twins by giving them twin-sounding names. I was once in a newborn unit in Chicago where there were six incubators containing three pairs of twins—Regina and Reginald, Marcus and Marcos, and Angel and Angela. Indeed, one study in the United States showed that 40 percent of twins were given "twin names." (This was more common with girls than boys.)

What many parents forget is that their twins may not always want to be seen as twins, let alone labeled as twins. (Fraternal twins will be as different as any pair of siblings.) Moreover, people are much less likely to try to distinguish two children called June and Jane than, say June and Mary. Recently, identical twins Kirsty and Kristy came to my clinic; those children are going to need very clear handwriting for the teacher to know whose essay she is marking. Even having the same initial can be a hitch to the teenager whose correspondence is private.

I believe that the two names should be very distinct. I say this even though a very different name can also bring its own problems. I asked a bright pair of 5-year-olds to write their names. Sam produced his triumphantly within a few seconds while Christopher struggled on with his for some time, looking demoralized.

The feeding regime with twins is a critical matter during the first six months, both for the babies and for the family's life pattern. Each family has to decide whether breast- or bottle-feeding the babies will be best in their particular situation. A clear advantage of bottle-feeding is that others, whether father, relatives, or friends, can share the work.

But there are other sides of the argument, as Plutarch was already declaring in the first century BC in *The Education of Children:* "Nature shows plainly that mothers ought to suckle . . . A wise thing is the foresight she has bestowed on women so that in the case of twin births she shall have two founts of nourishment."

However, despite this logical reassurance, many mothers doubt their ability to feed two babies at the same time. Few have ever seen a mother doing it. Even some midwives do not give mothers expecting twins the encouragement they need. Many mothers are made to feel that it will be a Herculean task and others get the impression that there must be little chance of success when they are gloomily told "well there's no harm in trying."

There is no doubt that it is often more difficult to establish breast-feeding with twins. Twin babies tend to be more premature than singletons so take longer to really suck well and thus encourage a good milk flow. It also requires a bit of juggling to start with to attach and keep two babies on the breast. But most mothers who have persevered feel that the early struggle was worthwhile. I have known many mothers entirely breast-feed their babies, some until beyond the first birthday.

I have known only three mothers who have entirely breast-fed their triplets, but many mothers of higher multiple births have happily partially breast-fed them all. The mother has fed one or two at the breast while someone else fed the others.

What are the advantages of breast-feeding? For a start, there are all those that also apply to single babies. Indeed, the protection against infection given by breast milk is particularly relevant to twin babies who are likely to be more vulnerable because of prematurity. There are two other considerations: first, a good deal of money is saved on baby milk; second, breast-feeding is the only way in which a mother can hold and feed two babies at the same time. Unless she has astronomically long arms she will not be able to actually bottle-feed her babies simultaneously. Very often both will be propped up and have no physical contact with the person feeding them. As nursing and cuddling time is always in short supply with twins this is a notable bonus with breast-feeding.

The crucial needs of a mother planning to breast-feed are preparation and encouragement. Before her twins arrive, it is helpful for her to visit another twin mother at home to watch her breast-feed and to hear how she manages. She can then see the techniques in action before trying herself. She can also hear from someone with personal experience about the difficulties and how they can be overcome.

There are many different positions for breast-feeding two babies at once—before and aft, crossed in front, both with legs behind, and so on. I know of six positions that are used, and there may well be others. Each mother will work out which suits her best and the position may change over time or for different circumstances. Some mothers prefer to feed the babies separately. For many this is easier. Others dislike being so exposed particularly if they want to feed the babies when friends and neighbors are around. Unfortunately, feeding separately inevitably takes nearly twice as long.

The clear advantage of bottle-feeding is that other people can share the workload (although there are always lots of other useful jobs they can do instead). The father, in particular, will feel more involved if he contributes to the feeding. On the other hand, once breast-feeding is really established there is no reason why the babies should not have the occasional bottle-feed to give mother a rest. She can even keep supplies of breast milk in the freezer.

Whether breast- or bottle-fed, each baby will have his own appetite and this must be respected. Too often mothers assume that each baby will have the same metabolism and therefore want the same amount of milk. Whenever James woke in the night and demanded a feed, Stephanie automatically roused Max and gave him one too. Max obligingly took the feed but he would have been equally happy left asleep. It was only when Max was clearly becoming a very fat baby that Stephanie realized her mistake.

As we have seen, twins are more likely to be born prematurely. Because of this immaturity and consequent small size, twins are also much more likely to need nursing in a Special Care or Intensive Care nursery. This is bound to be worrying to some degree and distressing for a mother who longs to have her babies as near to her as possible.

It can be particularly difficult, as shown earlier in the case of Sam and Fiona, if one baby is frailer than the other and therefore needs different nursing care. Some hospitals will recommend that the babies should always stay together even if one is perfectly strong and healthy. The stronger baby would then accompany his frailer brother or sister to Special Care and hopefully the mother can then be with both her babies. Some Intensive Care nurseries are unfortunately not yet equipped to have mothers staying on the ward.

If the babies do have to be separated it is vital for the mother to spend time with the ill baby, otherwise she may become so preoccupied with the baby by her side that at the emotional level she will "forget" the second baby in a far-off incubator. She may even feel that the baby is not hers and it will be much harder for her to get to know and love the child later.

The average birth weight for twins is about 5 pounds compared with 7 pounds for singletons and, as with singletons, boys tend to be heavier than girls. Fraternal twins tend to be a little heavier than identical twins. This may be because identical twins are more likely to be born prematurely and also because their growth may not have been quite so good in the womb if they shared a blood circulation (see p. 28).

Although in general twins tend to be smaller and frailer at the beginning, there are still many who are just as big and strong as single babies. I have known many pairs where both were over 7 pounds and a few pairs where they have been over 8 pounds each. The world record for twins is apparently a pair born in 1924 with a combined weight of 27 pounds 4 ounces—poor mother!

Sometimes newborn twins may be of very different sizes and, perhaps surprisingly, the biggest differences occur amongst identical twins. Differences in weight in newborn fraternal twins are usually because one baby had a bigger placenta than the other.

Differences in identical twins are often due to the twin-twin or fetofetal transfusion syndrome.

It was a pair of babies with the fetofetal transfusion syndrome (which can only happen in identical twins), that sparked off my interest in twins, (see page ix in the Introduction). The phenomenon arises when blood from one baby crosses to the other baby and the recipient doesn't give as much back. All single chorion placentas (see p. 9) have linking blood vessels or anastomoses through which the blood from one baby transfuses into the other. In most cases there is an even balance but occasionally the supply becomes lopsided. If this happens, the donor twin may become not only very anemic because he has given so much blood to his twin, but also very undernourished as a lot of proteins and nourishment will cross to the other twin with the blood. On the other hand, the recipient may become uncomfortably overloaded with blood.

It is not known exactly how often the fetofetal transfusion syndrome occurs but it is probably more common than currently realized, as minor degrees of transfusion might easily go unnoticed and cause no trouble at all to the babies.

The First Year

"I LOOKED AT THEM at their first birthday party and realized that I just hadn't had time to enjoy them, to play with them, and to cuddle them. Just keeping up with the feeding, the washing, the housework, had taken up every minute."

This was the sad comment of a mother with her first children, fraternal twin girls. Almost every mother of twins finds the first year hectic. Most appear to cope remarkably well but often at a high price.

Too many mothers feel they have failed if they seek or even accept help. One mother, Sarah, who lived on an attractive new housing estate in the north of England, was a perfectionist. When she heard she was having twins she was thrilled. The identical twin girls were a dream come true. She dressed them beautifully, always alike. Many of the dresses were exquisite but required hand-washing and ironing. If one baby was sick both were changed so that they remained in similar outfits. The house was kept as spick-and-span as the children. At the end of the first year Sarah was exhausted. She deeply regretted that she had not accepted the help that had been offered right from the start. By doing so she would have helped not only herself but the rest of the family. A less tired mother is nicer to live with and can cheer everyone.

Of course, the strain is much less when the father can be available for good stretches of time. Usually, however, he will be working in the daytime and possible working overtime to cover the extra expense of the second baby. Other help will then be invaluable. If useful grandparents are not available then there are many other possible sources of assistance. Some people will be able to afford a nanny, au pair girl, or some help with the housework. Others may find invaluable help through voluntary organizations. Teenage girls from the neighborhood may give useful assistance for one or two afternoons a week, perhaps to gain extra credit for a home-economics course. A nearby college may have students who want to do a project on twins and might be there to help for several days a week. The local social services may provide a home-help. If all these sources fail, the local Twins Club may have ideas about other possible sources of help in the area.

There are other ways to make life easier and finding the best means of transport is one of them. Transporting two babies is bound to be a problem for a mother on her own. In a study I did of twenty-three mothers, only one took public transport on her own before the babies' first birthday. And this mother only did it once: she couldn't face the bus journey home so she returned by taxi.

The choice of transport is important and each mother must think of her own particular circumstances before she launches into the huge expense of a stroller or carriage which may then prove unsuitable. One mother bought a beautiful, but very heavy, twin stroller which she then found impossible to push up the steep hill between the shops and her house. Mothers are constantly frustrated when strollers prove too wide to go through the necessary doors. Members of the local Twins Club are the best advisers on strollers and carriages and will often have good quality secondhand ones for sale.

Some mothers like to carry one of the babies in a sling while pushing the other in a single stroller. (A few strong ones carry both by this means.) A sling gives extra time for physical contact and the single carriage also makes walking in crowds much easier. One resourceful mother took three children on a large tricycle with the elder sister on the front and twins on the back.

It is essential that mothers should solve the problem of transport for their twins, not so much because the babies need fresh air but because the mother herself badly needs changes of scene to refresh her spirits and boost her morale. Once a regular outing becomes part of the pattern of the day the effort to get out becomes progressively less. But outings can rarely be hurried. Many mothers have told me how their shopping expeditions are prolonged by the well-meaning but time-consuming remarks of passersby. It is amazing how people seem to feel that there should be public right of access to twins. One mother resorted to putting a notice on her carriage saying "Please look but don't touch—I'm in a hurry."

Mothers who don't get out of the house will inevitably feel very isolated and the isolation can add to the other emotional strains of twin parenthood. I recently wrote strong letters to a housing department requesting rehousing for a mother who was on her own with her 6-month-old sons. She lived in a second-floor flat without a lift so she was unable to get the babies and the carriage downstairs without leaving one baby unattended. When she got downstairs the alleyway to the front door was too narrow to take her double stroller. She would sometimes go four days without leaving her flat or even seeing another adult. Architects and town planners are amongst those who need to be more conscious of the problems of parents of twins who at least temporarily need the same consideration that should be given to the disabled.

A study by Barbara Broadbent in Manchester showed that mothers with young twins left the house far less often than those who had one baby. A mother will also feel more isolated because friends may visit less. Many people are daunted by the idea of a hectic household with young twins. Some families with triplets have found that even members of their own family have withdrawn from the scene because they could not cope with the chaos.

Similarly, mothers of twins may be hesitant to visit friends. Coffee and a chat can prove an unnerving challenge for a mother who is trying to keep her eye on two active toddlers in someone else's precious, vulnerable, and hazardous home.

Even the most hectic and harassing day can be borne by the parents if followed by a good night's sleep. The sooner the babies get into a regular pattern the better. For some it seems to come quite naturally. Others may protest for many months. Twins vary greatly in how much they disturb each other. Some sleep through each other's cries, others seem to wake at their partner's first whim-

per. With twins it is all too easy for an intolerable pattern to become established.

Mr. and Mrs. J. came to my clinic bringing with them their
lively 2-year-old daughters, Lucy and Emma. Jane, their 5-year-old
sister, was at school. Both parents looked exhausted. They did not
need to tell me that sleep was the problem. Neither parent (except
the father when he was away on business) had had a whole night's
sleep since their first child had been born and now the parents did
not even sleep in the same room.

Each of the three children refused to be left alone until she fell
asleep. Often the parents had to lie or sit by the child until after
10 P.M. while she made strenuous efforts to stay awake to retain her
parents' attention. As the twins slept in the same room neither
could be left to cry for fear of waking the other. So, if one woke in
the early hours she would be taken into bed with one parent while
the other parent retreated to the child's bed. Now, to save disturbance in the night, the parents often started the night in this way.

Various efforts had been made to break this pattern but none
had been persisted with because even greater disturbance had resulted. But the parents now realized they simply could not go on
as they were. Together we devised a plan and they resolved to follow it even if the first nights were awful. They started with Jane.
At 5, she was old enough to talk sensibly about the problem and
to respond to incentives, not least praise. The first target was that
she should remain in her room during the night. A large chart
was put on her bedroom wall and she was rewarded with a star for
each time that she stayed in her room until an agreed hour. She
was given a large-faced and decorative clock with a marker at
seven o'clock. Another star was given if she went to sleep on her
own. Grandparents and teachers were told of the plan and they reinforced with encouragement. Incidentally, the stars themselves
were sufficient reward; they did not have to be translated into
treats of any kind.

Within two weeks there was an enormous improvement. The
parents then started with the twins. They put them in separate
rooms and decided to keep firmly to a pattern of putting them

down with a bedtime story and then leaving them to settle on their own. If protests persisted they would go back at intervals just to quietly reassure them but did not stay or pick them up. Gradually the children started falling asleep earlier. The same happened through the night. They remained wakeful children but they did learn to entertain themselves when awake and not to disturb the rest of the family. It was a painful process and one made more so by the parents having delayed the remedies for so long.

We have already discussed the importance of treating each twin as an individual from the very beginning. Many parents find that, although they are most careful about this themselves, they cannot easily persuade other people to do so. Even grandparents often seem to enjoy the identicalness of their grandchildren and may make little or no attempt to tell them apart. They may well diminish the potential individuality of the children by encouraging them to be dressed alike, often buying them identical outfits.

Some parents are not even aware of what is happening. I met a mother in the supermarket and admired her 6-month-old identical daughters. They were dressed alike and were, to me, indistinguishable. When I gently asked if people had any difficulty telling them apart, she replied, "No, Doctor, Jane has a birthmark on her bottom."

Any child has to find not only his own identity in relation to others but also his own individuality. Unless the child gradually learns what he likes and dislikes, he may become confused and unhappy. Moreover, he needs to learn that he has these and those strengths and these and those weaknesses. He should come to see that all of us are valuable. A child lacking a sense of his own individuality will lack a sense of his own value.

We still know little about how a child learns who he is but it surely must make it more difficult if, when he looks in the mirror, he cannot at once be sure that the reflection is of himself, not of his brother. Studies have shown that identical twins take noticeably longer to recognize their own mirror image than fraternal twins.

Being closely identified with each other from the start, twins have a special need to develop their individuality. The irony is that their twinship is all too often emphasized and even exaggerated. Having a special need to be treated as individuals, each is instead encouraged to see himself as one of a pair.

Parents and others do, however, enjoy the twinship and a balance has to be struck. Clothes of the same design but of different colors seem to make a good compromise in that the attraction of the twinship is retained while the children are clearly distinguishable, at least for that day. Different hairstyles can effect a remarkable change too. Some parents have felt the best way of ensuring that everyone knows who is who is to assign a certain color to each child, say yellow for one and green for the other. One family took the color coding so far as to name their children Jasmine and Emerald.

Mary, a primary school teacher, always dressed her boys in their own colors. William was in blue and Henry in red. Mary wrote to me when they were five saying she felt she had made a mistake in enforcing such a rigid color coding. The children had each become so attached to his own color that when they were offered chocolate biscuits wrapped in different colored paper they would only take those wrapped in their own colors. The green ones were discarded. More serious was the problem with an obligatory school uniform which included a blue pullover and tie. Henry was upset for many days before accepting it.

Clothes, however, are only symbolic. Much more important is the attitude of other people to the twins. They must learn to respect each twin as an individual just as they would any single child. Professionals are often as thoughtless as anyone. I heard of a surgeon who had arranged to remove the tonsils of one child and assumed that the mother would want those of his twin brother removed at the same time even though he had no symptoms. She did not. Indeed, even if both children do require the same operation I know that some parents would prefer them to be done on different occasions so that for a while each child can be given the special attention he deserves. Just as it is unfair for twins to have to share presents and surprises so it is not right to have to share sympathy and comfort.

All too often parents feel that twins ought always to be kept together. I have met 5-year-olds who have never been out of each other's sight for more than a few minutes. One pair of 4-year-old identical boys cried the moment they were parted. Yet they were soon going to be separated for hours at a time because one child, who had a hearing defect, had to go to a special school. For those children the parting would inevitably be painful as they had never had the chance to learn any independence or to have the confidence that, despite parting, they would soon be together again. Moreover, for twins who are used to being separated, time spent alone with their mother becomes a real treat and they will revel in the rare opportunity to have her undivided attention.

This lack of undivided attention and one-to-one communication is a problem for all parents of twins as well as for the children themselves. Many parents complain that they do not get the chance to relate wholeheartedly to one child at a time. Just as they are starting to attend to one twin, the other demands attention. Often they have to talk in a threesome. This triadic communication is frustrating not only for the mother but also for the child. Furthermore, it is almost certainly one of the reasons why twins tend to be slower to acquire speech than single children. To communicate satisfactorily, particularly with a baby, it is essential to have eye-to-eye contact. It is impossible to maintain this contact with two babies at the same time and one baby will soon lose interest in what the mother is saying.

Several studies have shown that mothers of twins cannot—inevitably—give as much time to their babies as they would to a single child. Esther Goshen Gottstein in Israel found that mothers of twins spent 35–39 percent of their time on infant-related tasks whereas the mother of one child spent 22–29 percent. As much of the twins' mother's time is bound to be spent on joint tasks the amount of individual attention a twin child receives will be even less.

A key problem is therefore how to distribute such limited attention as the mother can make available. Most mothers naturally plan to give equal attention to the babies, but it often turns out that one baby demands and takes more time—either because he cries a lot or because he's much slower to feed. The mother then feels guilty about the child that is being relatively neglected. She may also resent the one who is taking up so much time. The arrival of twins can have as profound an effect on the father as it does on the mother. For a start, he has a new and conspicuous image—as the father of twins—of which he is usually very proud. (Even though, as we discussed earlier, it is not the father's fertility that is responsible for the multiple birth!) Indeed, in my own study of families with young twins, I found that far more fathers than mothers were unqualifiedly delighted at the prospect of twins. Only one father out of the twenty-three was *not* pleased (he already had five children); although even *he* was heard boasting of his accomplishment in the pub.

In some families the parents will choose to share the care of the children equally although, in most, the mother will take the main responsibility. Occasionally it goes the other way and some men have given up their own jobs so that the mother can return swiftly to her job after maternity leave.

There are still, of course, many men who were brought up to believe that children and the home are essentially the woman's preserve. Unconsciously at least, they feel that the care of the twins should be entirely her responsibility. Such "macho" views are now being increasingly questioned and most fathers I have met in recent years have wanted to share in the babies' upbringing, or at least felt they should.

A father may at first be daunted by the prospect of coping with two babies at once particularly if one or both are either very small or frail. This trepidation is quite natural but it is vital that his confidence should be built up early on. The more he can be involved with the care of the babies in the maternity hospital and in the first days afterward, the better. (In jobs where paternity leave is not automatically provided, expectant parents should explore the possibilities with their employers long before the babies are born.)

The father will be deeply affected both by new emotional and unexpected financial pressures. His partner will inevitably be much more preoccupied and tired and he will himself serve a much more demanding role than he would as father of a single child. He may well have difficulty in sharing his time and energy between work and home. He will find that he is unable to devote himself fully to either babies, partner, or work. His work as such may seem harder and more stressful and his relationships with colleagues may suffer. Yet at the same time a feeling of guilt may well build up that, having to spend ten hours away from home every day, he may not be devoting enough time to helping his family.

On top of all this, the extra costs that twins bring can often mean the father having to work overtime. Moreover, as twins are so difficult for the mother to take around outside the home, he may also find that he has to do most of the shopping. The father could then be excused for thinking that these tasks were a sufficient share of the new burden but, unfortunately, he would be wrong. The twins are as much his progeny as the mother's and she is under huge emotional as well as physical—and organizational—pressure. She rarely has a change of scene, and is likely to have more interruptions of her sleep, especially if she is breast-feeding. The father can help not only by taking a regular share of the general domestic duties—especially at weekends—but also his share of coping with the nocturnal disturbances.

However, a father should not be thought of as just an assistant. The father's role in rearing any child is important in itself. With twins it is especially so. The extra demands created by the second baby plainly require his maximum possible participation. Moreover, as with all babies, each twin will need a great deal of undivided attention and this often depends on the other baby being taken off the mother's hands from time to time. The father's help is even more essential where there is no other regular help and in families where there are other children.

Once the expectant couple has recognized what they will both need to learn about in the first few weeks, they may be wise to reach a settled—if still flexible—understanding about who will do what, when. Both will then know where they stand and there should be less anxiety about what has, and has not, been done, leaving aside who should have done it!

Many fathers have been surprised and pleased by the ease with which they have taken on the nurturing role. Many who might not otherwise have had the chance because their partner did not "need" their help with a single child have been positively glad of the opportunity. And the results can be rewarding for the father. A study of preschool children in Canada showed, not surprisingly, that fathers of twins generally participate more in the day-to-day care of their children and as a result the twins were more attached to their father than were single children. When seeking attention, single children tended to wait until they could attract their mother whereas twin children tend to be equally happy to turn to their father and may indeed compete for his attention.

Inevitably there are problems. One father told me it was no joke when his triplets literally grabbed at him as he came through the door after a wearing day at the office. They fought and screamed because each wanted that cuddle or tickle or story, and wanted it alone. These scenes quite often ended in tears, he said. Other fathers have mentioned the dangers of social isolation. Although friendship with work colleagues continues, long-term friends tend to drop away. A father does not have the equivalent of the mother's network of other mothers but the now well-developed network of twins clubs can produce very useful father to father contacts. It is time much more attention was given to the father: the most effective forms of support and advice may often come from other fathers with practical experience.

Occasionally I have found the father becomes so deeply engaged in the upbringing of his children that he develops a role as a "twin expert." He may give so much thought and analysis to the children's special situation and upbringing that the mother feels overwhelmed. One father was so preoccupied with the development of his twin children as distinct individuals that every response to the children had to be considered in this light. It made the practicalities of caring for two children quite exhausting.

The father is, of course, particularly important as a gender role model to a boy twin in a boy/girl pair. As we will discuss later, such a boy may be overwhelmed by his more confident sister and time alone with his father will be exceptionally valuable. In this area as in others, the role of the father, not least in families with twins, needs more study. Only then will fathers receive adequate guidance and support in tasks for which their own families may have ill-prepared them.

Not all the difficulties are on the father's side. Some mothers find it difficult to give up their traditional female territory (most will be only too glad!) and need help in resisting becoming a martyr to the demands either of "motherhood" in general or the babies in particular. A father's resistance to doing his share may be less due to an unwillingness to play a nurturing role as such, than to taking orders from his partner. Someone who has never before been in an auxiliary role to his partner may at first find the new position uncomfortable. None of us likes taking lots of detailed instructions of the kind "Do this, now this, now the other," and it is far better to have a few substantial tasks to get on with, perhaps on a regular basis.

Of course, the mother may well find it difficult to give precise guidance. She is often groping in the dark in the early months, particularly if these are her first children. Her instructions to the father or other helpers may not be a hundred percent sound, and the methods she promotes one day may not work the next. Moreover, she may find the constant advice from relatives, friends, professionals—and even the father—inappropriate or misguided. Both parents can only hope to stay as patient and as receptive as possible to new ideas.

Life may not be easy for the older brothers and sisters of twins, especially for one who has been the only child. A child who has previously enjoyed the undivided attention of his parents for most of their waking hours may suddenly find them almost wholly preoccupied with the new arrivals. All children find it difficult when the second baby comes, but for older siblings of twins it is especially hard. They will lose not only much of their parents' time and attention but that of other friends and neighbors too.

Most parents are very conscious of the need to continue giving their older children special attention but other people can be extraordinarily insensitive. Close friends and relatives, let alone strangers, will rush up to a carriage to admire the twin babies without even acknowledging the older child. Sometimes he might as well not exist. One mother got so exasperated that she devised a seat for her toddler on top of the carriage so that no one could see the babies without greeting the toddler first.

Another mother described how a favorite aunt had come to tea and, as she left, thanked the mother for a "lovely afternoon." The 5-year-old then sadly said to his mother, "It was the twins that made it such a lovely afternoon for Aunty, wasn't it?"

Even within his own family this child can feel isolated. The babies are a pair, his parents are a pair, and he is on his own, the only singleton. He may use a doll or toy animal to pretend he has a twin. It can be helpful therefore to find a special partner for him too. It is no use finding another 3-year-old: best friends can be worst enemies a week later. But a godparent figure or a reliable teenager whose role it is to befriend this child can be invaluable. Treat outings, a "special postcard" or letter or just concentrating on him during visits instead of on the babies can do much to ease this child's situation. It may prevent him making the remark to his mother made by one 3-year-old when his twin sisters were 3 months old: "Mummy, I think it's time for the babies to go back in your tummy again now."

Careful thought must clearly be given to how best to prepare the older child for the double arrival. His importance as a helper should be emphasized. It helps if he can feel himself to be in partnership with his parents and certainly not just another of the babies. The idea that one twin is for mother and the other for him appeals to some children.

Much depends on the size of the age gap and the disposition of the older sibling as to how much of a helping role they will be able or wish to play. Whenever possible the help should be made interesting and amusing. No one needs another motive or incentive when the activity is fun.

Even a younger child can suffer from the extra attention bestowed on his or her twin siblings. An adult younger sister wrote movingly about her childhood feelings toward her attractive blonde twin sisters who were only 16 months older than she herself. "I struggled to understand my place in a family whose world revolved around two darling look-alikes. I was only known as 'the twins' sister.' " Their relationship with each other was complete and self-contained and beyond my reach. I felt lonely and angry."

Grandparents can be invaluable to parents of twins. They generally have prodigious advantages including genuine pride in and affection for the children, practical (if sometimes distant) experience of child rearing and (although some will still be working themselves) a certain amount of free time.

We often lament the passing of the neighborhood communities and the three (or four) generation extended families. But with an effort we can sometimes regenerate something of that situation and where genuine grandparents are not available there are sometimes "surrogate" grandparents—friendly neighbors who may be delighted to play a role. Nor will this help usually be regarded by them as a strain, a chore, or a burden. Our society tends not only to neglect its older generations but to undervalue the contribution they can still make. Many women who are past child-bearing age and, indeed, their partners, not only have much to give but will find considerable satisfaction in giving it. There can be a special quality to the care and love offered by a grandparent or the equivalent. They are often less hurried and therefore more patient. They also tend to be less judgmental and perhaps more obviously delighted to have the children's company.

Those who can offer more than spasmodic help may be most useful if they can offer a fairly regular pattern of support so that the parents can depend on it and plan around it. Some of the most invaluable help will be that which enables the parents to spend more, rather than less, time with the children, in an unflurried atmosphere. Nevertheless, the grandparents will naturally want time to themselves with the twins too, and often it will be of benefit all around if they take one out alone, and then the next time, the other. This enables both the grandparents and the parents to spend precious time alone with each child, thus reinforcing their individual relationships with each twin.

The Preschool Twin

··

THE PRESCHOOL STAGE is when the children become very conscious of being twins, with all the advantages of having an always ready playmate and all the hitches of always having to share objects and people, including their mother. The point at which twins become clearly conscious of each other varies enormously. Some very young babies obviously get comfort from each other, whereas others hardly seem aware of the other's existence until the end of the first year.

By the age of two, a child cannot avoid its twin. For some of them this is an especially difficult stage, one when any child will have lots of needs which are always urgent. He is deeply reluctant to share his mother and taking turns is not yet part of his understanding. Yet twins have to learn to wait at a much earlier age than single children. Mothers of twins not only spend less time with each child but they tend to respond less to sounds of distress and to bids for attention. Some twins will go to painful lengths to acquire a mother's undivided attention. Biting 2-year-olds are amongst the most regular clients at our Twins Clinic!

One mother was desperate. Each of her four children, the 5- and the 3-year-old and the twins of 2, felt he or she alone deserved their mother's attention. Each child was a delight on the rare occasions when she had one of them on their own, but the main problem was James and his biting. He would bite anyone he was with, but particularly Jonathon, his twin. And he bit with such ferocity that he drew blood. His mother took to carrying James about with her for the sake of the other children's safety, but this of course gave him precisely the special attention he was really seeking and hence served to reinforce his biting behavior.

Not surprisingly, Jonathon soon resented this attention to his brother and started biting too. An epidemic of biting now threatened. Somehow the children had to be shown that biting was not a worthwhile strategy—and without too much bloodshed *en route*. Boring them out of it was the only hope. Each time one started biting he was quietly and firmly lifted from the scene of action and held in a dull corner until he was quiet, then allowed to return to the others. The restraint was repeated immediately until the offender stopped biting. This strategy certainly reduced the number of bruises although it was many months before James stopped biting altogether. Sharp teeth are unfortunately one of the strongest and most effective weapons a child has and twins seem to use them to the full.

Disciplining twins can be unexpectedly problematic even for experienced parents. Many have been disconcerted to find how ineffective are the forms of control they had successfully used with their older children. Why is this? It is probably due to the support provided by the twin-partner. A child responds to discipline largely because he wants the love and respect of the person on whom he most depends. For most children that is a parent. But in the case of a twin the person whose respect and cooperation he most wants is by his side egging him on to worse and worse misdemeanors or demonstrating quite new ones. It is not therefore surprising that a parent needs to exert much more disciplinary pressure to have any effect. It has been found that parents have to use more overt verbal control and more reprimands to twins than to single children.

The pranks of twins can, moreover, be much more hair-raising than those of single children. With children of different ages one of them will be either sensible enough to foresee danger or physically incapable of performing the reckless act. Twins tend to push each other way beyond the limits that a single child of the same age would risk. Triplets show a further magnification of the problem, and it would be amazing if any house could be made quad-proof.

A further complication is that, because of their companionship, twins tend to have far greater perseverance. Twins will happily play for hours with the contents of their mother's makeup bag and I've lost count of the number of refrigerators that have been raided before dawn and the contents used with masterful ingenuity, usually on the least stain-proof furniture. One mother resorted to setting her alarm for 3.30 A.M. so that she could protect her kitchen from the inevitable invasion at 4.00.

Disconcerting habits may also be acquired which no child on its own could keep up. Rachel and Rebecca, a bright pair of identical twins, became known as the "whispering twins." It had all started when they were about $2^1/_2$ years old. When strangers appeared they would only talk in a whisper. This drew attention from both their parents and their friends as they tried to persuade them to break their silence. Initially the children would give in after a few minutes. Later they became increasingly skillful and determined, obviously regarding it as a challenge. By the time I met them at $4^1/_2$ years they could hold out all day and against all incentives including treat outings and much-wanted presents. Even their beloved grandmother, with whom they spent whole days, could not induce them to speak above a whisper. Indeed, they would sometimes actually announce to their mother their intention of not speaking all day. I cannot imagine a single child having the confidence and determination to perform such a feat.

The most tragic story of twins' combined determination to resist the normal influences of parents, teachers, and friends, must be that of Jennifer and June Gibbons, the identical twins portrayed in Marjorie Wallace's well-known book *The Silent Twins*.* This pair of West Indian origin were brought up in family quarters at the airforce base in Haverfordwest, Wales, and from their earliest years isolated themselves from the rest of the world. Even their own family had to communicate by letters pushed under the bedroom door.

The writing of stories and diaries was their passion and they did

---

*Penguin Books, 1987.

it at once intelligently and prolifically. In most other respects, however, they refused to communicate. Toward each other they had a fierce love-hate relationship. They were miserable if separated but had terrifying fights when together.

In their late teens their fantasy world apparently led them into real life orgies of sex and arson and they tragically ended up in prison. The lives of these highly talented girls show in extreme form the ruin that may ensue from twins failing to think of themselves as individuals from the start and relating as such to their family and wider community.

The twins' power over their parents can be increased by secret communication. Just as I remember as a child the tiresome habit my own parents had of breaking into (very bad) French in order that I should be kept out of the conversation, so many parents of twins feel excluded by the language of looks which can mean so much to a pair of 3-year-olds.

Preschool identical twin boys seem to be the most testing of all. Pat, a vicar's wife and herself a teacher, was near despair. She had always had an excellent relationship with her 7-year-old son but the 4-year-old twins, Peter and David, were quite different. It felt as though they were deliberately scheming to make life as difficult as possible for the family. They were inseparable, yet their every activity ended in vehement arguments and a fight. The noise levels were horrific. They were always getting into terrifying scrapes and took absolutely no notice of parental warnings.

Exhausted at the end of the day, Pat would look back and wonder if she had said a single positive word to the boys. Her vocabulary was almost entirely limited to "Stop that," "Don't do that," "IF you do that again . . ."

The boys had always been together—indeed they had never spent more than a few minutes out of each other's sight. Only their mother and elder brother could tell them apart; their father still had great difficulty. They were dressed alike which added to the confusion. Inevitably they were, to most people—"the twins." Rarely were they called by their individual names.

They talked at great speed but often their speech was incomprehensible to anyone except their twin. They had their own twin language. They also had some normal language, but it was immature as well as being hard to understand because of their poor articulation.

A plan was made to help the children to think of themselves more as individuals and for the mother (and father) to get to know each child separately. To start with they were to be dressed differently so that at least for that day everyone knew who was who. They were always to be called by their names and, at playschool, they had name badges so that the helpers knew immediately which was which.

Gradual separation was an important part of the plan. First Pat would take one shopping while the other helped father in the garden. Later friends would ask one out to tea while the other had a treat at home. Then they started going to playschool on different mornings, with one joint morning so Pat could still have a complete break.

Pat was amazed by the children she discovered. When they were alone with her each was a delight, amenable and fun. Discipline was no problem and they obviously enjoyed the new relationship with their mother. Their speech improved as they had more time alone with an adult. After a time their behavior, when they were together, also improved. They still had their arguments but they were much more responsive to their parents.

The "couple effect" of twinship described first by the French psychologist, Professor Rene Zazzo, can have both good and bad results. Cooperation between twins can accomplish tasks at a speed which two single children working together could never achieve. Nancy Segal, working at the Twin Study Center in Minnesota, found that this cooperation was much more marked, on average, amongst identical twins than fraternal. On the other hand, such cooperation may actually prevent some children from acquiring certain skills. If one always hammers the nails and the other cuts the wood neither may learn the other skill. Similarly with social or emotional skills, if one twin always greets people the other may be quite lost without his brother.

On the whole, preschool twins develop as well as single children. They actually tend to be more advanced in some skills such as sharing and interactive play. They have lots of practice. However, the one area of development which is recognized to be generally slower in twins, and particularly boy twins, is that of language. This has been shown in many studies. For instance Peter Mittler, a psychologist in Manchester, found that 4-year-old twins on average had a language level of $3^1/_2$ years. Dr. David Hay, from the La Trobe Twin Study in Australia, found that at the age of 30 months boy twins were 8 months behind singletons in their expressive language and 6 months behind in their comprehension. Mittler looked at the different aspects of language and found that the only area, linguistically, in which twins were ahead of single children was in "speed of response"—probably because they are so often striving to get a word in first. However, this race to get the words out can have a deleterious effect on their articulation: consonants may be omitted as well as the ends of words.

There are probably a number of reasons, both biological and environmental, why language often develops more slowly in twins. Twins tend to have more problems when they are first born and these may sometimes affect their long-term development, as suggested by a finding in the Australian study that twins whose language was delayed also tended to have less developed fine motor skills, such as manipulation.

However, there is no doubt that other factors play a part too. The environment in which a twin is brought up is inevitably different from that of a single child. First, they may have less opportunity to learn: busy parents have much less time to talk to their children. Mothers may also believe, mistakenly, that there is less need to talk to their children because twins entertain each other. Indeed, it has been shown that mothers of twins not only talk less to their children but use shorter and grammatically less complex sentences, and give less by way of reasoning and reassurance. This is scarcely surprising. One mother of 6-year-old triplets, herself a teacher, put it this way: "When the first one asks me a question I answer as fully as I can; when the second asks the same she gets a reply of a few sentences; the third is lucky if she gets more than a few words."

I have already mentioned the problem of triadic communication between mother and twins. Inevitably within this, one child may receive more language input than the other. It is understandable that a mother will talk more to a child who talks to her, if only to answer his persistent questions. A less vocal twin may well find he has less and less need to practice his speech as his talkative brother not only asks most of the questions to which they both want the answer but he also does most of the asking for many of the necessities of life. If one twin announces his need for a drink there is a good chance that both children will be offered one, not least because the mother won't want to be interrupted again ten minutes later.

In addition, there is the twin's characteristic problem of having a poor but strong model for speech—the other twin. With a single child the main model will usually be his mother or mother substitute. It will certainly be someone who speaks better than he does himself, perhaps an older brother or sister. A twin's main model is usually his own twin, who speaks as badly as he does. From a very early age their language becomes like the "Whisper Game": one child attempts to pronounce a word which is then repeated to and fro until it may bear no recognizable relation to the original. This is partly how the so-called "secret language" of twins develops.

This secret language, sometimes known as idioglossia or cryptophasia, can range from a normal language with such poor articulation that no one but the twins themselves can understand it, to such a profound distortion of both words and sentence construction that it becomes an elaborate language apparently quite unrelated to their mother tongue.

Many twins pairs, maybe as many as 40 percent, have a twin language at some stage. In itself it is not harmful as long as normal language is developing alongside it. It is only in the few rare cases where the twin language is the only language, that serious harm results. Koluchova described a pair of twins in Poland who had been virtually shut away for the first seven years of their life. When they were discovered by the child-care services they had no recognizable language but had their own elaborate oral communication.

The development of twins can also be held back by a relative lack of stimulation or opportunity. When I asked a mother how her bright pair of 2-year-old boys were getting on with feeding themselves, she said she had never let them try because it would make such a mess. They did not even know how to handle a spoon. In another case, 4-year-old triplets had no idea how to put on even a simple garment. To save time their mother had always lined them up in a row and dressed them herself.

Concerns about safety, however natural and necessary, also lead to twins missing out. Many mothers can cope in the kitchen and keep an eye on one toddler but most would feel it unsafe to have two. Likewise pastry-making may be fine with one 2-year-old but could easily cause chaos with two. Because of factors like this, twins seem to spend more time than singletons in playpens or confined to their cribs.

Opportunities do not necessarily mean active stimulation. Opportunities for peace, even solitude, may be equally important but are often difficult to provide for twins. One of the most harassing experiences is when a lively pair of 3-year-olds come into the clinic and start encouraging each other to explore their new environment. They become more and more frenzied with excitement and any effort by me to converse with one child is thwarted by the distraction caused by the other. Yet if either child stays on their own they are usually cooperative and peaceful. Except, that is, if they are so unused to being separated from their partner that they become miserably shy or start banging on the door demanding to join their twin.

I feel sure that twins have less opportunity for peace than other children. Many psychologists would argue that a measure of solitude is probably crucial to the full development of the personality and of self-awareness. Yet self-awareness cannot easily grow if the person concerned is constantly absorbed by relationships or bombarded by sensations.

Donald Winnicott as long ago as 1958 was urging consideration of the *positive* aspects of the capacity to be alone and the need for the child gradually to learn to tolerate longer periods of maternal absence without anxiety. He recommended that the infant should experience being "alone in the presence of the mother," stating that "The capacity to be alone thus becomes linked with self-discovery and self-realization; with becoming aware of one's deepest needs, feelings, and impulses."*

A parent may be impressed with this line of reasoning yet the practical difficulty for any mother of providing a growing child with the experience of safe yet rewarding solitude is very considerable. For a parent with twins the problem is plainly even more acute. Not only is the mother busier with domestic tasks but young twins actively compete for maternal attention. The mother can rarely find time to devote any kind of concentrated attention to one twin without the other twin calling either out of real need or out of jealousy. Moreover, when such opportunities can occasionally be found, the mother's (or father's) main objective will be to reassure the particular twin of his individual values and personality and hence to play with him in the ways he most likes, and to signal the specialness of the parent's affection. All these are very active processes and it is unlikely that the parent of twins will be unflurried and composed enough to create the atmosphere needed for a gently creative "alone together" solitude to emerge.

Furthermore, the twins themselves become hugely dependent on each other. They will generally spend more time together than with either of their parents. They therefore tend to copy each other or to react against each other: either way they are responding to *each other* rather than gradually and quietly discovering their own needs and wants—or at least learning to be contented on their own.

Certainly, no child is likely to spend less time on his own than a twin. Few twins ever sleep alone, wake alone, eat and drink

---

*The Maturational Processes and the Facilitating Environment, Hogarth Press, 1965.

alone, play alone, or meet others alone. Whether as friend or rival or antagonist, the twin almost always has a companion to fill a silence, interrupt a thought, or excite an action. Twinship and solitude are virtually antithetical, and perhaps more attention should be given to the psychological consequences of this unique kind of childhood.

Starting School

STARTING SCHOOL IS a major milestone for any child. For many it also involves the first prolonged separation from mother and hence the first experience of being alone. Twins are at a distinct advantage here; although they too must separate from their mother they still have the company and comfort of their twin. This is probably the reason why twins often settle more readily into school than single children. Another reason may be that they tend to attract friends, not necessarily by their social behavior and skills but because of their uniqueness as twins, which is often appealing to other children.

The question facing all families with twins is whether they should be separated in their schooling. Should the twins be in the same or different classes? Or even different schools? By the secondary school stage most people are agreed that it is better for twins to be in different classes, but when they are younger the decision should probably largely depend on how the children themselves are performing and the practical choices offered within the given school or area.

The first large-scale study on twins at primary school has recently been completed by Dr. David Hay and his colleagues in Australia. They found that about 30 percent of twins were separated in their first year and that this increased to nearly 65 percent by the fourth year. For a substantial minority the separation was not permanent, varying from year to year.

It was disturbing that 10 percent of schools said they had a fixed policy to separate twins. In 75 percent of cases the parents felt they had been inadequately consulted about whether or not the children should be separated. Parental reports on the children's reactions at home were often not taken into account and the twins themselves were rarely consulted about their views on separation. Contrary to popular belief the study found no convincing evidence that separation led to a better development of a twin child's individuality. They found that the benefits of separation were most evident when there were big differences in the abilities of the two children.

Some parents feel it is best for their children to start school in the same class and then, as their confidence increases, encourage separation. Many, if not most, twins will be in different classes by the age of 8. However, if the move to separate classes takes place after they have become established in school it is likely to result in one of the twins being parted not only from his twin but also from his friends while the other child stays securely with all the joint friends.

This difficulty can often be avoided through them having a period at nursery school or playgroup. There the twins can together get used to the break from their mother, and they may well be confident enough to go straight into different classes when they start school. In effect, they have a two-step introduction to functioning on their own.

Many parents are disconcerted to find how unaware some teachers seem to be of the particular problems faced—and created—by twins. Moreover, some schools have unfortunately rigid rules that twins must always be together or always apart. Most schools, however, are sensibly flexible and it is vital that parents discuss the school's policies and ideas about twins long before the children are due to start. Schools are often happy to take their cue from sensible parents since their own experience will be limited.

Parents and teachers alike must work on the assumption that each twin will want to grow up as an individual able to function independently of his twin, even though greatly valuing the relationship. In making the decisions about whether twins should be separated or not, the guidelines will be the children's happiness, their ability to perform to their full potential, and their development as distinct individuals.

. . .

In what circumstances will twins benefit from being apart?

If the children have different abilities, both may benefit from separation. Josh and Ben came to the Twins Clinic because their parents were concerned that Ben was becoming an increasingly withdrawn and unhappy child. The boys were 8-year-old twins, but didn't look like twins. Josh was big for his age—a good-looking, dark-haired, sportive child. Ben was small, fair-haired, and rather "weedy" looking. Josh looked several years older and no one would have guessed they were even brothers.

The children were in the same class. Josh was good at all the things that seemed to matter at school—games, reading, math. Ben avoided games whenever he could particularly if it meant playing with Josh, and he was several books behind in reading.

Ben had always had a vivid imagination. As a young child he would play and talk for hours with his make-believe friends. He loved drawing. But now that he was 8, little time was allowed for drawing and very little importance was attached to it.

It was clear that Ben was overwhelmed by his brother and, rather than compete, was opting out as much as possible. It was crucial that he should be allowed to be himself without constant comparison being made with his twin.

The parents searched the neighborhood and found a small school where a lot of individual attention was given. Little weight was placed on competition and there was a lot of emphasis on art and drama. Ben started there the next term. Within a few weeks he was taking a lead role in the school play, which his brother came to watch. There was a special art room where children could go in their free time and Ben spent many hours there; the walls at home became covered with his drawings. His parents couldn't believe the transformation. He became a happy, mischievous child who loved inventing new games, often at the expense of his brother. The children got on much better when they were at home and each enjoyed sharing their own different talents and news with the other.

By acting up together, twins' behavior can be not only distracting for themselves but may disrupt the whole class. Even the fact that twins have their own private form of communication can be disconcerting to others. Eye signals or nods may transmit a message (or answers to the teacher's question) from one to the other.

Nine-year-old James and Peter were always fighting. The fights started at home before they came downstairs in the morning, first over who should use the bathroom, then over who had the largest helping of Rice Krispies. Who should get the last kiss before school? Who should carry the letter to the head teacher? At lunch every chip was counted and if one had more than the other the whole dining room knew about it.

They were identical twins and only their mother could reliably tell them apart. Even she would make mistakes from behind. The boys were always dressed alike and very few people even tried to call them by their names, the usual forms of address being "Twin" and "James-or-is-it-Peter." They were rarely out of each other's sight, and as young children they had met few others of their own age. Their mother was busy with four children and was only too pleased when they entertained themselves. The boys became increasingly dependent on each other and at playschool they showed no interest in the other children. If one was ill the other refused to go on his own. At the same time the competition for their mother's attention increased in intensity and then the fights began. They couldn't bear being parted, but life was awful for everyone when they were together. Home was in turmoil and so was their classroom.

Although they always did everything together, James and Peter had a number of different interests. James loved swimming. Peter disliked the water but was longing to start the piano. A weekly outing to the swimming pool was arranged for James while Peter went for a piano lesson. When the boys were asked out, their mother specifically asked if just one could go and the other was given a treat at home. At first they hated this arrangement but each boy gradually began to see the advantage of sometimes having their parents' attention all to himself. The children started to dress differently at home. At school, where a uniform was compulsory, they wore a distinguishing initial. They hated the idea of being in separate classes, so they were parted only gradually. They began by being placed in different groups for certain activities but within a term were put into altogether different classes. For the first time they then began to make their own friends.

Identical twins will inevitably use their indistinguishability to play pranks on their friends and teachers. Which of us would not do so if we were given the opportunity? This sort of prank is usually just harmless fun, but if used to excess it becomes a considerable nuisance and hence another reason for separation. Again, any clear means of distinction can be helpful, such as different hairstyles. Sometimes even set uniforms can leave some room for individuality. For instance, one girl may be able to wear a gray cardigan and the other a jumper, or a skirt instead of a tunic.

As well as looking alike, some twins may actually want to *be* as alike as possible and hence to perform similarly also. This may result in the more able child actually performing less well because he wants to be like his less able brother. In such cases it is especially important to encourage the less able twin to develop any special interests or talents he may have and to show that these are highly valued.

Another problem for twins who are kept together is that their right to privacy is lost. Neither can choose what he will tell his parents about his life at school, because the other twin will often tell the story anyway. Reprisals often follow and hence conflict.

Jake and Reuben were fraternal twins, aged six. Jake was a quiet, conscientious worker who took school very seriously. Reuben was a less academic child who quickly got bored and then caused disruption in class. He was always being reprimanded. At first Jake was embarrassed but later became patronizing and would regularly come home to their parents with tales of Reuben's misdemeanors. Once the boys were placed in different classes, the problem was greatly reduced.

Sometimes twins will become too dependent on each other. Eight-year-old brothers came to see me. Whether I addressed a question to either of them, John always answered. Dean expected his brother to answer and never even tried to intervene. John was plainly becoming increasingly dominant and his brother more submissive. Once again gradual separation overcame a lot of the problem.

A similar picture can arise if one child matures more quickly than the other, particularly in the preschool phase and again in adolescence. This situation is more common in boy/girl pairs. In both these periods the girl may spurt ahead both physically and emotionally, and she may well start mothering her brother. He may not resent this, but it is not the way for a child to achieve his own individuality or to gain the respect of peers.

Any parents of two or more children may be faced with a dilemma when what is best for one child may not be so good for the others. They must decide not only what is best for each child as an individual but also what is best for all of them as a group. Joan faced this problem with her nonidentical triplets. At 7, Ben was obviously very bright. He was likely to get a scholarship to a highly academic private school. His brother Tom might also, with a struggle, be able to go to that school. That would leave Ruth alone at their present very good local primary school, where they were already all in different classes. Should all the children stay together, or should Tom go on alone? If positive reasons were found for Ruth to stay alone would it be best for both boys to go together?

In attempting to resolve such dilemmas one can only do one's best to balance up all the various factors.

There may be times when twins will benefit from being in the same class. As we have already discussed, young twins who are very close and have not been used to periods apart are likely to be happier if kept together at least until they have settled well into school.

Whether or not twins are separated, it is plainly vital that they should always be treated as individuals. Teachers need to be especially aware of this with identical twins. In order to treat children as individuals they must be easily distinguishable, called by their own name, and encouraged to develop their own interests and friendships. One teacher stressed the difficulty to me. She said every child in her small primary school was known by name not only to all the teachers but also to most of the children and the parents. The only exception were the Jones twins who were known as such—only their own class teacher ever used their first names. Inevitably that meant they were seen as a unit or, at best, two indistinguishable children who therefore had indistinguishable personalities. Their mother knew this to be far from the truth but could still not bring herself to dress the children differently.

While each twin needs to be recognized and treated as an individual both teachers and parents should avoid comparing them. One mother requested two separate appointments to see her twins' class teacher on Parents' Evening because she wanted to talk about one child at a time: a useful discipline for the teacher too.

Finally, some thought should be given to the position of any older brothers or sisters in the school. Twins often cause a sensation when they arrive at school: people are fascinated. It is not always easy to have your younger siblings as centers of attention or to be known mainly as "the twins' sister," and staff should be aware of this problem, ensuring that the children are known and respected in their own right.

Secondary School

SOME TWINS MAY benefit from being together through part of their time at primary school but by secondary school it is essential that a twin child has learned to function happily on his own. In the last chapter we discussed various situations which make separation particularly desirable. Some of these can become even more imperative at the secondary school stage and additional reasons may also emerge.

Some twins find security in being seen as twins and, as we have already seen, this is often reinforced by their parents' obvious pride in having twins. They may themselves want to look alike, even when they are not identical. This not only impedes the development of independence but may prevent a teacher giving each the appropriate kinds of support.

I have met secondary school teachers who are deeply concerned by their inability to tell the twins in their class apart. It is particularly difficult if the two children have quite different abilities and personalities and therefore need different approaches from their teacher. No teacher can treat a pupil with sensitivity if she always has to ask his name first. Teachers have described the adamant refusals of some parents to allow even the slightest distinguishing feature of dress or hairstyle, when these could so easily and unobtrusively overcome the problem.

Surprisingly, even teachers themselves can neglect the importance of twins being treated as separate personalities. A bright pair of 15-year-olds were doing a field project in their geography class. The teacher gave every member of the class a different project but automatically gave the twins a joint project. They were indignant.

Problems can arise if constant competition becomes painful to one or both twins, or results in one of them opting out.

Fourteen-year-old Sophie and Carol were star divers. Their bedrooms were overflowing with trophies and press clippings. Yet every competition ended in unhappiness: they could not both win. The loser sulked, the winner was exuberant. Their parents were torn between wanting to congratulate the winner and knowing this would distress the loser. Both children suffered. For several years the triumphs were at least evenly balanced, but gradually Carol pulled ahead until it was rare for her to come second. Sophie became increasingly disgruntled and finally gave up diving altogether.

Other twins would undoubtedly say they had achieved more through being a twin. Timothy Knatchbull movingly described his relationship with his identical twin, Nicky, who was killed at the age of 14 by an IRA bomb, together with his grandfather, Lord Mountbatten. The boys were both pacers and runners across a broad range of activities. As one led so the other would be stimulated to work harder until he took over the lead. This can work very well when twins are of similar ability.

Ross and Norris McWhirter were another such pair. (Tragically, Ross, too, was killed by an IRA bomb.) As a pair they undertook many ventures, such as compiling the *Guinness Book of Records*, which neither would have taken on alone. As journalists, when one was reporting from overseas the other could receive a telephone message with the key facts and then compose the piece—the speed of report was an editor's dream. They also enjoyed many competitive sports together.

The delightful identical twin bishops, Michael and Peter Ball have also clearly gained much support and fun from each other in their chosen career. Presumably identical twin sportsmen such as cricketers Alec and Eric Bedser, runners Susan and Angela Tooby, and tennis players Tim and Tom Gullikson must also have found it convenient as well as motivating to have an opponent and constant training partner so readily at hand. However, the experience of the Gulliksons demonstrates yet again how people assume that twins should always be treated as one; when each member of the international tennis team was given a car for their use it was assumed that the twins would only need one between them.

Cooperation has obviously been beneficial in these families and there is no doubt that many twins can help each other. Yet this help must not result in the masking of either child's difficulties. Big gaps in the understanding of one or both twins could be missed if homework is always done as a cooperative exercise. Many identical twins have, however, been falsely accused of colluding because of the similarity of their work; it has often been shown that identical twins writing their exams in different rooms can still produce almost identical answers.

Each child should be allowed his own moments of glory and also of privacy, for example, when in disgrace. Whether good or bad, school reports should be read by parents alone with each child. It should be up to the individual child himself whether he shares the contents with his twin. Similarly with examination results, parents should congratulate (or commiserate with) each child as he reveals his results, and not immediately ask the other what *he* got. They should wait until they are alone with the second child before raising the subject if he has not chosen to do so before. Comparison of examination results is all too easy to fall into but can be unnecessarily painful. Such comparisons will only encourage the misleading assumptions that twins either ought to compete or ought to be alike.

As mentioned earlier, twins will often develop at different speeds and at different times both emotionally and physically. Occasionally even identical twins will do so. The differences often become most marked at puberty, and particularly in boy/girl pairs. Both children may find the discordant development difficult to handle and for some pairs of twins this could be a good reason for them attending different schools.

It may sometimes be necessary for school authorities to make special concessions for twins. Strict regulations may have seriously deleterious effects. As young children James and John had been inseparable. At primary school, teachers and parents had worked together to encourage their independence. Gradually they each made their own friends and by the time they were ten they were quite settled in different classes and happy to separate for outings. However, problems arose when plans were made for their transfer to secondary school; because the twins happened to live just on the other side of a boundary, they were due to go to a different school from most of their close friends.

The boys were naturally very upset. They started alone at their new school. Shy by nature, the boys stuck together like limpets. As all the children went through those difficult early stages of making new relationships and friends James and John stayed together and just looked on. Many children felt intimidated by this pair of inseparable identical boys—a phenomenon they had not previously encountered. Few attempted friendship and the boys became more and more isolated, thrown in on their own cocooned relationship.

Another example of special concessions being advisable for twins is shown in the case of identical twins, Jeremy and Alexander. During the last two years at primary school it had become obvious to the boys and to everyone else that Jeremy was finding school work much easier than Alexander. At first Alexander had tried to keep pace. Then he gave up and just opted out—often not bothering to put any effort into a task and, whenever possible, getting Jeremy to do it for him. It was obviously essential that the boys should be separated and go to different secondary schools.

Although the local school, only half a mile away, would have been suitable for Jeremy, the one that could give Alexander the individual attention and encouragement he needed was fifteen miles away. The practical difficulties of having two children so far apart would have been enormous. As there was also an excellent school for Jeremy in the same town, this seemed the solution. However, it took many months and a huge volume of paperwork to persuade the education authority that twins do often deserve special consideration.

Long–Term Growth and Development

....

"ARE THEY GOING to be small?" "Will they be slow?" Many parents of twins have asked me anxious questions like these. It seems to be widely believed that twins will not develop physically and mentally as well as single children.

Parents can be reassured: nowadays the great majority of twins grow and develop as well as their singleton peers. Indeed, recent studies have shown that even those who start very small, catch up remarkably well.

Of course, there are many twins who have actually excelled in all sorts of walks of life, both together and individually. I have already discussed the McWhirter twins, who compiled the *Guinness Book of Records*, and Peter and Michael Ball, the bishops. David and Michael Thorne are both generals, and Peter and Anthony Schaffer are playwrights. Some centuries ago Romulus and Remus are reputed to have founded that great city, Rome, and Cosmas and Damian, a Turkish physician and apothecary, respectively, were celebrated patrons of medicine and pharmacy in the third century. The previous speaker of the British House of Commons, Bernard Weatherill, is a twin. There have been several famous sportsmen and women, including the Mahre skiers, and the boxer Henry Cooper, as well as the Bedser cricketers, the Gullikson tennis players, and the Tooby Olympic runners, mentioned in the previous chapter. Sometimes both twins will excel but in different fields. The Medvedevs are an example; Zhores is a well-known scientist working in London and his twin, Roy, is a notable professor of history and dissident working in Moscow.

Earlier studies have shown that adult twins are slightly smaller on average than the general population. A survey in the 1950s of Swedish male army conscripts showed that twins were on average 1.3 cm shorter than their single counterparts. This is a very small difference. Moreover, now that premature and very small babies are better nourished during the early crucial months, present day twins may well have made up the deficit. A large study of twins in Louisville, Kentucky, showed that twin children had caught up in height by the age of 4 and in weight by the age of 8. Another study compared the growth of twins with that of their parents and siblings. This showed that there was very little difference in height between twins and their families but twins tended to be lighter and therefore thinner.

Fraternal twins tend to become less alike in size as they grow older whereas identical twins tend to become more alike. Even those identical who were of very different weight at birth often become similar in build later on. The pattern of growth in identical twins also tends to be more alike: their "spurts" and "lags" usually coincide. This is particularly noticeable at times of rapid growth such as puberty (see below). In fraternal twins, one child may suddenly race ahead of the other whereas identical twins will lag or race ahead together.

"Will he catch up with his twin?" This is what every parent inevitably asks when one baby is born much smaller than the other. Unfortunately the question is not easy to answer. Some smaller babies catch up remarkably well and quickly. Joseph and Sam were such a pair. Although identical twins, Joseph weighed $3^1/_2$ pounds when he was born, Sam weighed nearly 6 pounds. But by 18 months there was only 5 ounces between them and by the time they were 8, Joseph was actually half an inch taller.

On the other hand, Laura and Susan, also identical twins, who weighed over 7 pounds and $3^1/_2$ pounds, respectively at birth, retained a considerable difference in weight, and Susan never caught up. They were both healthy little girls with similar abilities but at the age of 7 Laura was sturdy and of average height whereas Susan was wiry and petite, being 3 inches shorter and 10 pounds lighter than Laura.

Both these pairs were identical twins so why should the outcome have been so different? The key may be the length of time the smaller baby had been short of nourishment. We are now learning from ultrasound scans that differences in growth may start really quite early in the pregnancy. We also know that the fetofetal transfusion syndrome (see p. 28) may arise as early as the third month. Perhaps Joseph had been short of nourishment only for the last few weeks of pregnancy, by which time he had already acquired the potential to grow well, whereas in the other pregnancy, Susan may have been getting less nourishment right from the start so that she was never able to develop a potential equal to her sister's. Only further research will resolve the many outstanding questions of this kind.

The intellectual development of twins is broadly similar to that of single children except quite often in the area of language (as discussed in chapter 5). Most studies have shown that the great majority of twins have intelligence well within the normal range even though the average level in twins is a few points lower than in single children.

There are several possible explanations for this small disparity. As we have seen, twins are more likely to be premature and of low birth weight and both are known to carry a risk of learning difficulties. Furthermore, it is well established that children born close together in a family tend to be at an intellectual disadvantage. This applies to the younger and the older child and may be due to the smaller amount of parental attention that each child can receive. No spacing could, of course, be closer than twins.

This leads on to the critical question of whether being brought up as a twin is, of itself, a disadvantage? This is hard to judge, but the results of one study which compared the intelligence of a group of twins with that of children who had lost their twin at birth, and were therefore brought up as single children, showed that the latter tended, on average, to perform better. This was even though many of these single surviving twins had had more problems as babies. This study suggests that being brought up as a twin is the detrimental factor rather than just being born as a twin.

Nevertheless, the differences are not, as I have implied, substantial enough to worry about. All these research findings emphasize the need for parents and teachers to give special attention to the complications of twinship and to compensate for those that are disadvantageous.

With their intelligence levels, as with their physical growth, identical twins tend to be more alike than fraternal twins. Fraternal twins perform less and less similarly as they grow up and in the end are no more alike in their intellectual skills than any brothers and sisters. Identical twins, by contrast, tend to have their "spurts" and "lags" at the same time, as with their physical growth.

In identical twin pairs of different birth weight, the smaller twin is usually at a slight intellectual disadvantage. Often, however, the actual difference in school performance is less than would be expected from the difference shown in the results of intelligence tests. This may well be because the smaller child has had the constant stimulation of a more able twin.

Differences in physical development within a pair of fraternal twins may become very apparent during puberty. The normal age for the onset of puberty varies greatly so it is not uncommon for one twin to have a spurt in growth several years ahead of the other. Sometimes the difference can be very disconcerting for the smaller twin who may then find themselves being regarded as the younger brother or sister.

Occasionally the earlier onset of puberty for one can redress a balance. Liam and Mark were fraternal twins and for the first twelve years Mark had been the taller and stronger child. Strangers always assumed that Liam was his younger brother. The boys tended to live up to this expectation, to the detriment of Liam who remained immature for his age and dependent on Mark. At 13 Liam entered puberty, ahead of his taller brother, and within a year he grew 5 inches, overtaking Mark. As his physique developed, so did his self-confidence. Two years later Mark had his own growth spurt and finally ended up 2 inches taller than Liam. This did not matter. Liam had had the opportunity to develop his confidence and that endured.

Identical twins usually enter puberty at about the same time and it is not unusual for identical girls to have their first menstrual period within a few days of each other. However, there are exceptions to this and I have seen identical, as well as fraternal, twins where one had a growth spurt two years ahead of the other. In one case I met of identical twin boys, this was a strange experience for them both. Having been almost indistinguishable for thirteen years they quite suddenly looked no more alike than ordinary brothers.

Girls tend to enter puberty earlier than boys and therefore to have their growth spurt sooner. Similarly, they tend to become more responsible and work-oriented earlier. This increase in size and maturity is often accompanied by a bossy "elder sister" attitude to a twin brother which can be undermining for him. During this period it may well be better for boy/girl pairs to be separated both at school and in many of their other activities. Boys particularly can benefit from time alone with their father who always plays a critical part as masculine role-model (whether consciously or not) in the development of the boy's personality.

Independence

···

THROUGHOUT THIS BOOK I have discussed ways in which the individuality of twin children can be encouraged. The ultimate aim is for each child to become an independent adult, able to make their own choices and to realize their full potential. They need to come to regard their twinship as a bonus but not as a relationship or status essential to their value as individuals or to their personal fulfillment.

Adolescence is a crucial phase in the development of independence. Twins have a double process to work through: they must become independent not only of their parents but of each other. Some may delay the second process and later find it an even more difficult one.

Similarly, the parents have to work through a double process. Not only is adolescence a time for separation from each child but also for starting to lose their special self-image as parents of twins. When their children go their own ways the loss of this prestige for parents can be painful. Outsiders often find this puzzling, even surprising, but this special sort of pride is very powerful in many parents of twins.

There are other situations which may add to the complexity of twin adolescence. It is, for example, a time when youngsters are very conscious of their individual appearance and this can clearly pose a problem for identical twins who are frequently mistaken for each other. Some pairs of twins will go to great lengths to make themselves look different and sometimes take up extremely different images to do so more completely. The punk hairstyle, earrings, and leather jacket may be partnered with a conventional suit and tie. Other pairs may wish to look different but find that their basic taste is so similar that their efforts are confounded. There are many stories of identical twins who have gone shopping in different towns and returned with identical garments. Even twins who have been separated for most of their lives may appear at their first reunion dressed in similar outfits.

One child may outshine the other, as in earlier years, through a greater degree of confidence, but in adolescence the difference can become even more conspicuous when one twin is obviously more attractive to the opposite sex.

Mary was a tall, elegant 15-year-old who enjoyed parties and going around in a group. She had lots of friends and was obviously attractive to the boys. Her twin sister, Alison, was small and dumpy. She was naturally shy and preferred to do things alone or with a special friend. She did not want to join in her sister's social life but at the same time found it hard to cope with being left out and the feeling that Mary's friends felt sorry for her. When they left school and each started a job where they were not even known to have a twin sister, the situation became much easier. Alison quietly made her own friends and developed her own interests.

Both twins, or perhaps just one of the pair, may realize that a separating of the ways is essential to preserve the identity of each partner. One adult twin, normally very competent in the world, found that if she spent more than a few days back again with her sister she lost all her ability to make decisions. She lost herself and her self-esteem.

Other twins, particularly those who have not been encouraged to spend time apart in the early years, may find parting so difficult that they keep putting it off, making it all the harder in the end.

I first met identical twins Jean and Janet, when they were 28. They had always been very close and were now trying to be more independent; the wrench was proving agonizing. They were the youngest of four children. Their father had died when they were young and they were always very close to their mother. They had been popular at school and were never short of friends but always saw each other as "best friend." They were always known as "the

Twins" and many people could not tell them apart. They did everything together and it was never suggested that they should spend even as much as an afternoon apart. They had played together for hours on end without any disharmony and they could hardly remember an argument, let alone a fight.

The two sisters later went to the same university. It was not until then, at the age of 19 that they even considered spending time apart. At that point Janet suggested they should live in different houses. Jean reluctantly did so but felt desolate and lost. As does sometimes happen, it was Jean—who had often seemed the leader as a child—who found the separation hardest. Janet seemed to cope perfectly well on her own, while Jean lost weight and had all sorts of other symptoms for which no physical cause could be found. She went home for a term and then tried to start again, but still could not cope. Eventually she left the university and went to work in another city.

Both girls then developed close relationships with boyfriends and for several years all went well. However, when Janet's relationship broke down she then became very dependent on Jean for support. Two years later Jean's relationship with her boyfriend also finished. The twins migrated back to each other and they started sharing a flat. Then Jean panicked; the same dependency was developing. She moved away again, was utterly miserable and had many hour-long telephone calls with her sister discussing her misery and how much her life was being ruined.

Meanwhile they met up with another pair of identical twins who had had similar problems, but with even worse results: they had both become addicted to alcohol. This was such a warning to Janet and Jean that they sought help immediately. As Jean had recognized, they were really going through a delayed and prolonged identity crisis of the kind that many adolescent twins go through earlier and less dramatically.

This case illustrates in a fairly extreme form so many of the joys, trials, and pains of the twins' relationship while they are growing up and when they eventually part that I have asked permission to quote some passages from the account one of them wrote about the experience. The broad outline of their story has already been given but it is the depth of feeling involved that I hope will come across from the discontinuous fragments of Jean's writing that follow.

It is only now since I am able to look back that I realize that being an identical twin sets one in a completely different "life path" to other individuals. Right from the very beginning one does not come into this world as a single being, but with a constant companion and the two of you grow together, getting constant support, companionship, and guidance from each other.

One of the biggest differences as a young child growing up as a twin was that there were never any moments in our entire day that one was alone ... I cannot ever remember daydreaming or thinking about myself. We were "growing" together and there was no time for any introspective thoughts.

Up to the age of 13, I cannot remember one instance of us being apart from one another. Going to boarding school we were put in the same dormitory. Again we were known as "the Twins" which made making friends fairly easy. People did not really know us as individuals as we were always together.

The one difference between us and the other children was that quite a few school friends (aged 16) were beginning to have boyfriends. Janet and I never had any as we got all the companionship we wanted from our own relationship . . . [Later,] having a relationship with someone other than Janet was an extremely odd situation as there had been so few instances when I had ever been on my own, that suddenly having to communicate with someone else seemed difficult.

Until we were 19 no one would really have known us well as separate individuals. When we went to the same university we were put in the same room but through mutual decision we decided that we would move into different cottages and try and experience life on our own for the first time ever. I dreaded it . . . How could I explain to anyone that I was now experiencing something so completely new that it was terrifying . . . I felt completely cut in half. The feeling ten years later is so vivid that I can remember it precisely . . . I experienced the terrifying realization that on my own I felt so lost and bewildered that I was unable to project myself as the Jean that they knew. I felt a complete stranger to myself . . . Buying food for the house was a nightmare of wandering around the food store completely lost.

For a few weeks I covered up and kept up an act of being happy and then, one evening at a disco, I could go on no longer and as I was sitting with friends I just started to cry and cry uncontrollably. I was driven back to Janet's cottage where I thought I was dying. I could not breathe. How I got through that dreadful night I will never know. The next morning I was able to talk to Janet and explain how I felt. I was no longer Jean and Janet but now Jean on my own, but I felt like no one on my own.

The following three years were ones of complete confusion. It was a matter of learning who I was and being responsible for the first time ever for my own reactions or at least being conscious of them. When Janet had been around I had known myself so well (she was like a reflection of myself). But on my own I was not anything.

Every day was odd. Being on my own was the most isolating feeling possible. I felt totally unprotected and for the first time really responsible for my own actions, what I said, who my friends were. It should have been like a new birth but it felt like death . . . Most of the time over the next three years I felt very odd and lost . . . there were times when I wanted to be dead although my love of life made me persevere as during all those previous years I had always been so happy. So I knew what real happiness and security of a wonderful relationship was like. I had had it all my life. I had never suffered the difficulties that most individuals surely suffer.

.   .   .

I am sure that Jean's experiences are not uncommon even though to many people they will seem almost incomprehensible. However, much of the pain could probably have been avoided if, as children, each had had more chance to be independent. Jean agrees with this so strongly that she is now eager to talk to parents of young twins, so they may learn from her experiences. She advises them to encourage their children to have times apart and to make their own friends from a very early age.

A sad situation occurs when one twin values the twinship more than the other and invests more in it. A simple example was given to me by a 16-year-old girl who was enormously proud of her twin brother. She would introduce him to all her friends as "my twin brother" whereas to his friends she would just be "my sister."

The difficulty was demonstrated in another pair whose friends and tastes were fundamentally different. One would have been content to meet occasionally at their own family gatherings whereas the other wanted to include her twin sister on every possible occasion, always proudly introducing her as "my twin."

For many twins, the usual progression to relationships with teenagers of the opposite sex works very smoothly and may well facilitate the necessary separation from their twin. For others, however, it can be more traumatic. If only one of a close pair develops a new relationship, the other may feel rejected and deserted. It may also be the first time that a pair have not shared every secret. There have been extreme examples where, for example, one twin girl suffered from such severe depression that she committed suicide when her identical twin announced that she was getting married.

Occasionally there are difficulties when a boyfriend or girlfriend of one twin becomes attracted to the other twin. This seems to happen relatively infrequently and many pairs have an understanding, often unspoken, that there will be no poaching of partners.

Some twins, particularly identical girls, have found that the opposite sex is put off by the closeness of their partnership. Some boyfriends are jealous of the strong relationship with which they have to compete, and show definite hostility toward the other twin.

I have already mentioned the problems arising from the differing pace of emotional development, particularly between boys and girls. It is sometimes very galling for a boy twin when his twin sister starts going out with older boys who appear to regard him as a sort of younger brother. In other cases boys may have a proprietorial attitude toward their twin sister and be suspicious of the motives of the young men with whom she goes out. Many of them, in all fairness, will just feel protective and want the best for their twin, as might any brother.

As with singletons, the majority of twins will eventually marry. In the past, several studies have shown that some groups of twins are less likely to do so. Sir Francis Galton was the first to notice this in the mid-nineteenth century. Professor Rene Zazzo in Paris confirmed his finding, and found that it was the females who were more likely to remain single. More recent studies, however, have not shown nearly such big differences between twins and singletons and Dr. Kallman, in the United States, found no higher proportion of single women amongst American twins.

In some ways twinship may be a good preparation for marriage in that the potential joys and harmony of a partnership are better appreciated—as well as the capacity to handle the inevitable stresses and strains. In other ways, however, twinship may lead to exaggerated expectations. A newlywed twin may be surprised and disappointed when her husband fails to understand immediately and instinctively in the way that her twin did. Explanations which would have been superfluous for a twin now become essential.

Some parents worry that the special relationship of twins may be spoiled if the children spend time apart. I feel sure this is not so. For many twins their relationship is enhanced—they often appreciate each other more when they have spent some time apart.

There can be no stronger indication of the power of the twin relationship than that demonstrated by many reunited twins. Many twins who have been separated soon after birth have searched relentlessly for their lost twin. Others who did not even previously know they had a twin, have developed a deep and almost immediate friendship following their reunion. Several reunited pairs have actually decided to live together, others have taken up jobs together.

One of the most dramatic stories is that of the American identical triplets, Bobby, Eddy, and David, who were separated in infancy and adopted by three families who lived many miles apart. Nineteen years later, a college friend of one of them was surprised to meet someone who he thought was his friend even though he knew he had left the college the previous term. After a period in which he and the second boy doubted their sanity, the truth emerged and the identical brothers Bobby and Eddy, were reunited.

The *New York Post* was attracted to the story and published a photograph of the two boys. Number three, David, saw the picture and soon the trio met. A firm friendship developed and the triplets now run a popular restaurant together.

Several pairs have first learned that they were twins when some stranger has greeted one of them in a surprisingly friendly way. Occasionally twins have just "bumped" into their mirror image. Some who were adopted in infancy have accidentally discovered they had a twin when searching birth records to identify their mother. In some of these cases the need to find the twin becomes even greater than that of finding the parent. No one knew more about the intensity of the feelings involved than the late John Stroud, a social worker in Hertfordshire, England, who was responsible for helping a large number of separated twins to find their partner, sometimes across the world. Some years ago I attended a lunch where he was the guest of honor among thirty or more reunited pairs. I was deeply moved by the occasion.

Many of the pairs have been astonished by the similarities of their life histories and of their behavior. An American pair, Jerry and Mark, who met in their thirties, discovered that they had both become firemen and drank only Budweiser beer. They also found themselves making the same remarks in chorus.

Daphne and Barbara arrived at their first meeting after thirty-nine years each in a beige dress and a brown velvet jacket. They had both met their husbands at the age of 16 and gone on to have two boys and a girl following a miscarriage. Another British pair, Bridget and Dorothy, met each other wearing seven rings and found that one had a son called Richard Andrew and the other a son called Andrew Richard.

Jim Lewis and Jim Springer were separated as babies and met nearly forty years later. Each had married someone called Linda and then someone called Betty. Both drove Chevrolets, chain-smoked Salems, enjoyed stock-car racing and took their holidays on the same Florida beach.

Even those twins who were brought up extremely differently showed some surprising similarities. Few can have had more different upbringings than Oskar Stohr of Germany and Jack Yufe of California. Separated soon after birth, Oskar was brought up by his grandmother in Germany, went to a Nazi-run school and became a member of the Hitler Youth movement. Jack was brought up by their Jewish father in Trinidad and later worked in two kibbutzim in Israel. Despite all this they each had neatly trimmed moustaches, stored rubber bands around their wrist, and read magazines from back to front. Both also had a habit of sneezing loudly in public to provoke a reaction.

How many of these strange similarities are due to chance and how much to their shared genes?

Nowadays, at least in the UK, twins would rarely, if ever, be separated for adoption. A generation ago such separations were not uncommon and twins who were separated at or soon after birth provide a unique and unrepeatable opportunity for studying the relative effects of genetics and environment on every conceivable aspect of life from metabolism and growth to intelligence, personality, and temperament. Professor Thomas Bouchard and his colleagues at the Minnesota Center for Twin and Adoption Research are carrying out an extensive study and have already investigated over one hundred sets of reunited twins, including many from the UK. They compare the reunited identical twins with identical and fraternal twins who have been brought up together and to fraternal twins who have been reunited. The results to date are inconclusive, but are showing that the degree of genetic influence varies greatly between the different areas studied.

10

The Disabled Twin

···

As with single children, so with twins: a small proportion of them will be disabled either physically or mentally or both. The precise incidence of disability in twins has not yet been calculated but all the evidence suggests it is definitely higher than in single children.

This is not surprising. We know there is, on average, a greater risk of disability among children who are born prematurely. Disability may also occur following certain conditions unique to twins such as the fetofetal transfusion syndrome (see p. 28). In addition, there used to be an increased risk of brain damage in second-born twins due to lack of oxygen during labor. As we have seen, this is no longer the hazard it used to be in developed countries, but remains a serious one in other parts of the world.

Abnormalities in development will often be detected in twins earlier than in single children because the mother is made more aware of the defects of one child as she watches the progress of the other. This early detection can be very valuable in ensuring prompt treatment or remedial action.

Pat had identical triplet boys. They were all equally bright and responsive and she would probably not have worried about Jack until much later had she not noticed a significant difference between him and the other two. These two were sitting on their own and starting to crawl at 8 months whereas Jack still had a very curved back when he was pulled up to sit and was only just beginning to drag himself across the floor. Pat also noticed the stiffness in his legs when compared to his brothers. These were the first signs that this little boy had cerebral palsy.

Clarissa noticed the difference in her twins during the first week. Rebecca was alert and active from the start: Barnie was sleepy and felt floppy. Nor could she persuade him to look at her, even for a few seconds. It later turned out that Barnie had an abnormality of the brain which was to cause slow development.

Genetically inherited abnormalities like cystic fibrosis, chromosome abnormalities like Down's syndrome, or defects like spina bifida probably occur with the same frequency in twins as in single children. Fraternal twins, as with brothers and sisters, are unlikely to both be affected. Even pregnancy infections, such as rubella (German measles), or fetus-damaging drugs such as thalidomide, can damage one baby yet spare the other.

Perhaps surprisingly, it is relatively unusual even with identical twins for both of the pair to be affected, except in the case of genetically inherited disorders. I have seen identical twins where only one of them has Down's syndrome. This is presumably because the chromosome abnormality developed *after* the fertilized egg had split. Different chromosome patterns are also the explanation for the rare occurrence of identical twins who are of different sexes (Turner Syndrome) which is described on page 2.

Throughout this chapter I refer to the "disabled" twin and to the "healthy" twin. I do of course recognize that the "healthy" child, like all of us, will have some disabilities (he may not be able to draw or to sing in tune), and that the "disabled" child may otherwise be perfectly able to do many things. I use the terms in the conventional way for the sake of brevity and only with these important qualifications.

Any parent of a disabled child has to come to terms with a whole lot of mixed emotions, not least a kind of loss: the loss of a perfect child. For parents of twins there can be felt to be an added bereavement, the loss, as it seems, of the twinship. All parents are proud of having twins and usually like people to think of their children as twins. For some parents it can be hard to stop treating the children as twins and thereby relinquish the image. Yet for a child to be treated as a twin to someone who shares neither the same mental nor physical age can clearly create an added burden to one or both children.

Anita and Angela were the fourth and fifth children in the family. Anita had been born without difficulty but Angela got stuck and after an hour of exhausting pushing by the mother a caesarean section was performed. By the time Angela was born her brain had suffered irreversible damage from lack of oxygen. She did not breathe on her own for over half an hour despite every effort at resuscitation. When she did start breathing it was obvious from the start that something was very wrong. She became increasingly stiff and had frequent fits.

When I saw her at the age of 8, Angela was an attractive little girl sitting in a wheelchair. She could not even sit up on her own. She smiled responsively and made noises but she could not say any recognizable words and appeared to have very little understanding. Both her mental and physical age were still that of a baby. By her side was her healthy twin, Anita, dressed identically.

One otherwise sensible mother almost refused treatment because of her wish for the children to be kept looking alike. Catherine and Elizabeth were 3-year-old identical twins. Elizabeth, the second born, had, like Angela, undergone a difficult time when she was born and now had mild cerebral palsy. The physiotherapist had advised that she should have a built-up boot to help her walk. Initially her mother refused as it would mean that, for the first time, the children would not be in identical outfits. Soon, however, the mother realized her mistake and the boot proved a great help.

Encouraging and praising the two children appropriately can be difficult. George was a bright 3-year-old who was severely disabled by cerebral palsy. For many months he had been struggling to crawl. Finally he managed to get up on his knees and unsteadily crawl across the sitting room floor. Both his parents showed their delight and showered him with praise. His twin, Sam, could not of course understand what the fuss was about. After all, he had been walking, never mind crawling, for ages. And nor, certainly, did he remember receiving the same praise for similar feats. When he now tried to attract the same attention from his parents by vigorously crawling and clowning he was ignored.

It is not uncommon for siblings of handicapped children to regress in their development and imitate their disabled sibling during times of stress. To have a handicapped sibling is difficult for most brothers and sisters. Inevitably the activities of the family will be curtailed and the extra time needed to care for the disabled child must mean that some of the mother's, and the father's, time is diverted from the healthy children.

A healthy twin child will suffer no less from these problems and his feelings may be magnified if he is constantly reminded of his twinship. He may also feel guilty, however illogically, that he was spared. This has to do with the well-known "survivor syndrome" affecting people who survive natural or man-made disasters. He may feel especially guilty if his own good health was secured at the expense of his twin. He may, for instance, have received a larger share of the available nourishment before he was born. This feeling of guilt sometimes induces the healthy twin to try somehow to make amends by taking on some of the burden of caring for the disabled one.

Michael and Peter were identical twins. Their parents were thrilled with their healthy babies and no one but their mother could tell them apart. When they were 9 months old, however, both babies had an attack of gastroenteritis. Peter became severely dehydrated and had convulsions. As he recovered from the gastroenteritis it became apparent that he had suffered brain damage during the illness. He could no longer sit on his own, he was very floppy, and his previous laughing and babbling was reduced to the occasional reluctant smile.

As the months went by, the differences between the twins increased. At 18 months Michael was running around, while Peter was just starting to crawl. By 3, Michael was chattering with full sentences while Peter could say only a few words. By 6, no one would have known they were twins (except that they were always dressed alike). Peter was much smaller and it was obvious that he was mentally retarded.

I first met the family when the boys were 13. Their mother came to see me because she was concerned about the healthy child, Michael. Academically he was doing well at school and was in the top stream for all subjects; he was hoping to become a doctor. He was quiet and conscientious and his school reports were exemplary. The concern was that he would never join in any extracurricular activities. Although he enjoyed sports he never stayed on after school to play games. He declined school outings whenever possible and, despite encouragement from his parents, refused to go on a five-day trip to France. He rarely played with neighboring children at the weekends. Instead, he would hurry home to spend all his spare time playing with and caring for Peter. Was this the only way he could find to ease his guilt?

Another frequent cause of curtailment in the healthy twin's social life is his embarrassment at being seen with his disabled sibling, and friends may be discouraged from visiting the house. This problem is less likely to occur if the twins are less obviously treated as twins. The emphasis on the twinship can be more embarrassing than the disablement as such.

Even as a baby, the disabled child is likely to be much harder to look after. He may be a difficult or a slow feeder; he may have fits. The mother will usually therefore need to concentrate on him and any passing friend may be given the healthy baby to feed. Friends are often apprehensive of handling the disabled child and yet the parents would be delighted if someone else would learn to help so that they could, at least sometimes, enjoy caring for the healthy twin. They could then feel confident about occasionally leaving the child in the care of a friend while they had time away from home with the healthy child.

The disabled child will often need specific therapies and the speech therapist, the occupational therapist, or the physiotherapist—or all of them—may become regular visitors and hence special friends of this child. Frequent visits to the hospital will mean lots of special attention for one child whereas the other will just trail behind or be left at home with a neighbor. The healthy child will often feel unnoticed. Some will strive for attention in a negative way, making as much nuisance of themselves as possible; others may show their insecurity by clinging to their mother and refusing to talk to anyone else.

At times, even the most sympathetic child is bound to feel jealous and resentful of the attention given to his disabled twin, who may seem to have too many concessions made, such as being let off household chores and instead expecting to be waited on. He or she may even seem to get extra treats. The healthy child can display feelings of resentment or rejection in many different ways, sometimes in overt jealousy, and at other times in more complicated behavioral disturbances.

Catherine, whose identical twin, as I mentioned before, had mild cerebral palsy, showed her unhappiness when she was 7. At school the teachers had noticed that Catherine had become very quiet and withdrawn. She rarely spoke and would often go off on her own in the playground. At home her behavior fluctuated between open hostility toward her mother, when she would resist any physical contact, and frank demands for a cuddle or to sit on her knee, often at the most inconvenient times.

There were three other children in the family, an older brother and a younger brother as well as Elizabeth, her twin. Her father was a market gardener so her mother was very busy helping with the flowers and vegetables, as well as looking after the four children. Hard as the mother tried, it was impossible for her to give the children the individual attention she would have wished. The youngest did quite well because he was at home each morning, and Elizabeth inevitably had times alone with her mother when she went for her special treatments or did her daily exercises.

The only occasions that Catherine had any prolonged time alone with her mother was once a year when she went for a checkup at the hospital. This was then made into a treat afternoon with shopping and tea, which she loved. Ways were therefore found so that the mother could leave the other children at home on one afternoon a week and take Catherine along to the swimming baths. Catherine loved swimming but more important, she loved being alone with her mother. It was also a very relaxed way for the two to have easy physical contact and made something of a break for the mother. At the same time, Catherine was learning a skill and was delighted to take home her first proficiency badge, which was just as warmly received at school.

When one of the children is disabled there are, of course, practical restrictions on the activities of the family as a whole. In the case of the more physical activities this is obvious; hiking holidays are unlikely to be appropriate. But if one child is mentally retarded, then some museums, the theater, or cinema may be ruled out for family outings.

It can be very hard for both twins in an identical pair when one of them is disabled. Each can see what they might have been like. Even in pairs who are close friends it must inevitably be difficult to watch your twin sister accomplishing feats that will always be beyond your own grasp. When a sensitive 17-year-old in a wheelchair heard that her sister had gained a place at university she quietly said to her mother, "Jane's future is all bright and clear while mine is in darkness." However great the pride and delight of the parents, their joy in the success of the one child is bound to evoke sadness for the other.

There are, however, positive aspects to the situation for both the handicapped and the healthy twin. The handicapped twin has the stimulation of a more able model continuously by his side. Later he will have the great advantage, not only of having the friendship of a normal brother or sister, but also that of their friends. Meanwhile, the healthy twin may develop an understanding and sensitivity that he would otherwise not have had.

It is not uncommon for people who have experienced disability in the family to go into one of the "caring" professions. Parents will often have to strike a precarious balance between encouraging the child to follow his caring inclinations and seeming to encourage his feelings of guilt.

I have concentrated on the problems that arise if one twin is handicapped and the other not, partly because this is the more common situation and is less well understood. Where both children are disabled, however, parents do have an enormous burden. Not only do they suffer the double tragedy and bereavement but they also have to sustain the sometimes enormous emotional and physical demands that two disabled children continue to make.

If both children are deaf, as might happen following a rubella infection in the womb, the individual attention essential for them to develop normal speech and learn to lip-read can prove impossible for a busy mother to provide, particularly if she has to give attention to an older child.

When both children are physically disabled, the physical demands alone can be overwhelming. Joan, herself a nurse, had twins, Ben and Jane. Both had severe cerebral palsy and when I saw them at the age of 5, the only way they could get about was by "swimming" across the floor. They couldn't manage steps and their bedrooms were at the top of a steep flight of stairs. Father worked unpredictable hours so Joan usually found herself having to carry both children up and down the stairs. The strain on her was enormous and she was already having treatment for her backache.

A crisis was averted by the arrival of a volunteer for three mornings a week from a local parent-support organization. Not only did this provide practical help for Joan but equally important was the close friendship that developed between herself and the volunteer. As so often happens, many of the friends that Joan had had before the children were born had drifted away. Sadly, some had just felt they could not cope with the stress of the household, and isolation had added to Joan's burden.

All families with a disabled child deserve ready access to whatever help they need. With twins, practical help is a key factor. Only granted this kind of assistance can the mother give the disabled child or children the necessary attention and treatment and also have time alone with her healthy children.

Many mothers will feel isolated. In particular they may miss out on the support that parents of twins would normally receive from their local twins club. Many parents find it very painful to see and mix with healthy twins. On the other hand, they will enjoy and get support from sharing their experiences with others in a similar situation. They are often helped by joining groups specially for families with disabled children and many will have a country-wide network of contacts as well as a newsletter.

A pioneer Special Needs Clinic is run by the Multiple Births Foundation in London where families can come to talk not only about their disabled child but also about the needs of the healthy twin. Fathers often play an active part in this. Often the lunchtime meeting where all the families meet each other and can talk to volunteer parents who have similar personal experiences can be as valuable as their discussions with the pediatrician.

The Death of a Twin

"How lucky that you still have one lovely baby!" or "Well, it would have been hard to cope with two!" These are the thoughtless remarks that every parent who loses a newborn twin receives time and time again. No other parent would be expected to find comfort from the death of one child in the survival of its sibling. Parents who have lost a twin may even be made to feel ungrateful about their surviving child and therefore guilty about their grief.

Because the babies are of the same age, many people seem to imagine that, in some peculiar way, one of them should be dispensable and the other a sufficient replacement. Yet each baby is, of course, a complete and precious being in itself. For most of her pregnancy the mother has been relating to both or all of her babies, however many there may be. And a death is a death, even if the lost baby be one of quads or more.

Although most twins will remain alive and well, the number who die is inevitably higher than with single children because many more twins are born prematurely. Moreover, the greater the number of babies in a multiple pregnancy, the greater is the risk of miscarriage or very premature birth. In 1987 the whole of Britain mourned with Mr. and Mrs. Halton as their septuplets, who were born seventeen weeks early, died one after another during their first two weeks.

As we discussed in chapter 1, many twins are lost early in pregnancy—the vanishing twin syndrome. The developing baby dies and is reabsorbed by the mother's body. In the old days, and probably in most Third World countries still, a mother need never have known she had conceived twins. The only tangible indication might have been a small bleed from the vagina early in the pregnancy.

There have been occasions when a mother has thought or been told by the doctor, that she has had a miscarriage and then, to her surprise, she finds she is still pregnant. This is probably the explanation for the stories of impossibly large babies being born very prematurely. One mother had a miscarriage at eight weeks. Seven months after the miscarriage she delivered a vigorous, healthy baby of 8 pounds. There was no question of this baby being the ten-weeks-premature baby expected by the doctors: it must have been the surviving twin to the baby that miscarried seven months before.

It is well known that if a mother becomes pregnant again very soon after she has had a stillborn baby she may emotionally confuse the two babies, the dead one and the new live one. Twinship can provide an extreme example of this confusion when one baby dies before, or soon after, birth. The mother is faced with the unenviable and complex psychological situation of mourning the death of one baby while she celebrates the life of the other. Faced with this impossible combination of emotions, many mothers postpone their mourning. Some mothers, however, find they cannot attend to their living baby because of the intensity of their grief for the dead one.

A mother who is not able to grieve adequately for her dead baby while caring for the live one, will often feel guilty about her unfinished business. She wants and needs to grieve but cannot make enough emotional space to do so. One mother, Rosemary, herself a doctor, came to see me fifteen months after the birth of one twin and the death of the other. They had been born twelve weeks early. Jane, the second born, weighed just 2 pounds and died after a few hours. The other baby, Sarah, weighed 2 pounds and was very ill for many months. Her survival was touch and go. She spent ten weeks on a ventilator to help her breathe. During that time she had a hemorrhage into her brain which later caused a blockage of the fluid around it so that she developed hydrocephalus—an abnormally large head. She had to have a series of operations to reduce the pressure in her head.

When Sarah finally came home at the age of 5 months, she needed a lot of extra care including physiotherapy from her mother twice a day. Rosemary's thoughts and days were filled with the concerns and practicalities of caring for this frail child. There was still no room to think about her lost daughter, Jane, and this worried her. She needed to give her love to Jane too, if only to say a proper good-bye to her. Arrangements were then made for Sarah to be looked after for three days so that Rosemary could go away peacefully and concentrate on Jane, to think about her, to mourn for her without interruption. After this, the grief remained but she felt less confused and frustrated.

When the opposite occurs and the mother is unable to tear herself away from the dead baby, the live baby may well be neglected and even rejected. Sometimes a mother will react like this when people do not allow her to express her grief. She may desperately want to talk about the dead baby and, if not allowed to do so, may silently idealize the dead baby (her "angel baby"). This in turn alienates her from the survivor, especially if this baby is difficult to nurse.

The father's reactions often embody the same contradictions and are more bottled up. Furthermore, the reaction of the two parents may be quite different, sometimes leading to stress on their own relationship. One parent may not allow the other to grieve as he or she wishes, either by refusing to grieve or, sometimes, by grieving so inconsolably that the other parent feels they have been left no scope to express their own grief. Many fathers, and some mothers, are apt to think it "morbid" to think or talk about a death. Fortunately, people are learning that it may be healthier to do so, to express feelings and not to suppress them.

Most people do not, of course, find it easy to talk about a dead baby and relatives and friends often go to great lengths to avoid mentioning it. With the death of a twin it is especially easy to do this because there is another baby to talk about. By concentrating on the live baby it is quite possible, beyond the delivery room, for the dead baby never to be mentioned again. This can be profoundly harmful. The parents have a right, and in a sense perhaps a duty, to grieve for so sad a loss. Moreover, a bereavement that is not worked through by both parents may have damaging results, sometimes much later.

Even professionals, who should know better, can collude in pretending nothing untoward has happened. Maureen and her husband, John, had been thrilled at the prospect of twins and were fortunate in attending a hospital whose policy was to allocate one particular midwife to a mother throughout her pregnancy. The midwife had shared the couple's eager anticipation of twins and had become a close friend. Unfortunately this midwife happened to be on leave for the weekend when Maureen was admitted in labor at thirty weeks. The babies were born but the second of them was already dead. When the midwife came back on Monday morning she was horrified to hear what had happened. She hurried to see Maureen who was in a side ward. She spent ten minutes admiring the healthy baby; she never once mentioned the one who had died. It was only because other patients told Maureen that the midwife had been in tears as she left the ward that Maureen ever knew that she cared at all about the death of the other baby.

However, in partial defense of the midwife, we must remember that she became warmly attached to the couple concerned and she, like many medical staff, might have gone through a recent series of tragedies in her work. Medical staff are not only human, they feel deeply responsible for much of what happens and can sometimes feel their professional competence to be under threat.

The loss of one or more babies in a higher multiple set can be particularly difficult. After many years of treatment for infertility, Pat and John had very premature quads. One by one during the agonizing first three weeks the three boys died. Samantha, the only girl, struggled on. Pat was devastated by the death of her precious boys. John discouraged her from talking about them. He refused to take her to visit the graves. He kept on saying, "We mustn't spoil our enjoyment of Samantha by thinking of the boys." Pat felt increasingly guilty as her thoughts became more and more filled by the boys. She felt she needed to give special time to her sons, to talk about them and to create memories of them. Only then would she be able to concentrate on Samantha and love her whole-heartedly.

If the couple is left with two or more babies it is unlikely that they will get much sympathy from other people. Sheer logic seems to say that their hands are full enough and that it may have been just as well that the number of babies has been reduced. Yet to the parents each of the babies has been precious. A mother of two surviving triplets told me she made particular efforts never to look harassed or untidy (and made extra visits to the hairdresser), as she dreaded people saying, "Three would have been too much for you to cope with."

Again, professionals are not always as understanding as they should be. One couple who conceived triplets as a result of infer-tility treatment were initially horrified at the prospect of three ba-bies, but by the time the babies were born they were thrilled and after two had died they were heartbroken. They were therefore deeply hurt by a thoughtless remark of the gynecologist when he said, "You asked for one baby and that's what you've got." Any im-plication that the death or deaths might have been all for the best, even if objectively this might be thought so, can be profoundly hurtful to the parents, and can indeed produce a justified anger.

It is hard to grieve for someone when you have few memories and few tangible reminders of them. But memories can be preserved and even created and these can be of enormous help to parents later on. For a start, it is imperative that parents spend time with their dying baby. Too often they are encouraged to give all their at-tention to the healthy one. But they will have years and years to give their love to him; they may have only hours or days to care for the ill baby and they will gain lasting comfort from the knowl-edge that they gave all the love they could to this baby in the brief time available to them. Moreover, if she has had the chance to really know the baby who died, a mother will find it much eas-ier to clearly distinguish the two babies in her mind later. There is otherwise the danger of her thinking of the surviving baby, as one mother put it, as "only half a baby" and of not being able fully to grieve for the dead one.

Naming the dead baby is always important but especially so in twins. Not only does it make it easier for the parents to distinguish the babies in their thoughts and when they talk about them, but for the survivor, later on, it is obviously much easier if he can refer to his sibling easily and naturally by name.

For many parents it is vital that there should be a proper and memorable funeral service and an individually marked grave or memorial to their baby. Later this may also be important for the survivor to have a special place he can visit on anniversaries or birthdays.

One mother who had lost her twin daughters during the twenty-second week of her only pregnancy was still distraught three years later and quite unable to continue her work as a writer. She had not actually seen the babies and had no mementos of them. No X-rays or other mementos were obtainable from the hospital. Substantive memories were then deliberately created for her and her husband by having a memorial service at which the priest baptized the babies *by intent*. The baptism certificates were treasured by the parents. Three months later the mother had resumed her writing career. In part, perhaps the very validation of her feelings and the public sharing of them in a solemn ritual had helped to clear her way forward.

The value of an image of the twinship is strongly felt by many mothers. It is, I think, vital, however poor their condition, that the babies become real to their parents by being named, held, and photographed. Photographs should perhaps become as natural a part of death as they are of life. Many parents treasure their photographs of their dead baby. These images provide precious mementos of both the baby and the twinship. When it has not been possible or appropriate to photograph the babies together, an artist's sketch of the two together may be made from two separate photographs.

Even where one or both the twins have died, most parents want to know if their twins were identical. There are several good reasons for this. First, it is natural for any parents to want to know as much about their own babies as possible, not least because it helps them to imagine their dead child. The survivor is also likely to be interested as he grows up. It will, of course, be important to know if the baby has died from a disorder that might be inherited. Knowing the zygosity will also give the parents a clearer idea as to whether they are likely to conceive twins again. (Those with fraternal twins will have a greatly increased chance, unlike those with identical twins.)

It must again be stressed that a mother who has had a multiple pregnancy continues to think of herself as a mother of twins (or more) whether or not one or more has died. Many mothers who had a higher order birth deeply resent the labeling of their surviving children as, say, "twins" when they were born as members of a triplet set.

One mother demonstrated her need to be seen as the mother of twins when, while shopping with her 18-month-old surviving daughter, she met a mother with a carriage containing identical twin girls of the same age. She spontaneously said to this woman, "I've got twins too." "Oh," replied the other mother, "and where is your other little girl?" "At home," the bereaved mother replied.

Many parents of singletons, or people with little knowledge of twinship, will inevitably think this mother's reaction wrong, even absurd. They could well feel it was unnatural or at least excessive, even self-indulgent. Relatives and friends of twin parents can only admit that here, too, there may be something of a mystery and ask for understanding. Certainly the pride of being an expectant mother of twins is enormous and the failure so narrowly to become one is therefore all the greater. One mother of a 2-year-old surviving twin said to a group of similarly bereaved mothers—almost as a confession—"I think I am coming to terms with Charles's death. I shall never come to terms with not being a mother of twins." All present agreed.

Following the loss of a twin, some parents may care well enough for the surviving baby but may be unable to really celebrate it.

One couple who would normally have had a child baptized in infancy were unable to face the ceremony until it was suggested four years later that the service should include a memorial for the stillborn twin. This they could accept.

Although a mother (or father) may damagingly suppress her grief for many years, it is probably never too late to resolve it. At the age of 22 a nurse who was a surviving twin showed her mother an article in a nursing journal describing the difficulties faced by parents who lose a newborn twin. For the first time this mother realized that the powerful feelings with which she had been struggling for so many years were neither unique nor strange.

Her husband had never mentioned the stillborn boy since the day of the birth but when shown the article he gradually talked more and more about his son. Together, with the surviving daughter, they then sought out the site where their baby had been buried, a communal grave. Later they held a small memorial service for him. The relief to the mother, the father, and to the family as a whole, was enormous.

A peculiarity of the present law in England makes it especially difficult for parents who have a stillborn twin before twenty-eight weeks and a second baby who is alive at birth (whether or not he subsequently survives). By law, one is a miscarriage and the other a baby. Clearly this is absurd, emotionally, but this failure to acknowledge the first baby officially as such can cause great pain to the parents.

The sudden unexplained death of an infant, otherwise called a "cot death" or "crib death," also occurs in twins. It used to be thought that twins in general were more vulnerable to it than single infants. Recent studies, however, show that the increased risk is confined to premature and low birthweight twins. Very occasionally both babies will die at the same time or within a few days of each other. Presumably the same undiagnosed infection has attacked both babies.

The inevitable guilt and the bewilderment felt by parents who have been through a cot death is sometimes intensified by others failing to recognize that the cause of death is genuinely unknown. They insist on asking, "Yes, but what was the *matter* with him?"

Fortunately, friends will usually more readily appreciate the loss represented by a cot death than the death of a newborn twin. However, the loss of one twin may very naturally lead to an overwhelming parental fear that the other twin might also die. It is therefore not only a wise precaution but a big reassurance to the mother if the baby can be taken into hospital under close observation for a few days. The mother of twins who loses one of them suffers no less than a mother who loses a single baby, but she does, at least, have the other baby to preoccupy her, not a huge vacuum. The pattern of feeding, bathing, and diaper changing must go on. There is still a baby who needs her love and will respond to it. Nevertheless, sometimes the presence of the other baby may in some ways increase her pain. A mother may put all her care and love into her surviving child while still yearning for the lost baby.

Twins are no more likely to die in later childhood than single children but when they do it can be devastating for the surviving twin. The loss of any sibling can be deeply disturbing for the survivors but the special closeness of relations between twins makes for a very special sense of loss. The surviving twin's behavior at such a time can disrupt family life; and parents may honestly but deeply disagree about the best way to help their unhappy child. The marriage itself may suffer so it is vital that such families find support and counseling.

Most mothers have ambivalent feelings toward the surviving child whatever his age. Some overprotect, others reject, some do both—perhaps to conceal the rejection from others and indeed from themselves. The mother often comes to idealize the dead twin and forgets that he too could sometimes be untidy, naughty, and disobedient. She may also feel that the survivor was somehow responsible for the death. Perhaps he had an unfair share of nourishment before he was born? Or had he distracted her at the crucial time? Had he actually caused the accident that killed his twin? Occasionally, of course, one of these things might be true but where the fault lay, if anywhere, is not the main point.

With identical twins, especially, the parents may be haunted by seeing the dead child in the living twin. Sometimes the one will look distressingly like his dead brother or sister and even adopt mannerisms that were previously performed by the dead twin. These recurring reminders of the lost child have sometimes been so painful that mothers have temporarily rejected survivors and devoted their attention to their other children or other concerns.

In some societies fathers are too often expected to hide their grief. They are supposed to get on with their work as usual, give quiet support to their partner and leave all the crying to her and the rest of the family. This can plainly be an intolerable strain since he too will be feeling the loss, particularly perhaps of an older child. Sometimes their dreadful sense of loss can be even greater than the mother's, and so can their anger. The father too needs support and comfort and to be helped to express his feelings, even if he may not be fully aware of the depth of emotion that has been stirred within him.

By meeting other men who have suffered similarly a father will soon realize that there is nothing to be ashamed of in expressing grief, anger, and all the other possible emotions, whether in words or in tears. None of us is as strong as we sometimes pretend. And what sort of "strength" is it that bars one from showing that one is not made of stone?

Most fathers are naturally proud of their twins and the loss of one of them can induce the father to reject the survivor as being, without his twin, somehow incomplete. Some such fathers have insisted on removing all photographs of the twins and become unable to relate to the surviving child. This is clearly a serious situation for the whole family and professional help is needed as soon as possible. It may help if the father at least realizes that the phenomenon is not uncommon and can be remedied, albeit sometimes slowly.

There will, of course, always be various painful reminders of the twin and of the twinship, as there are in any bereavement. As the surviving twin starts, often nervously, on each new stage of life, like playgroup or school, the parents will long for the companion that should have been there to share the new trials and adventures. Anniversaries such as birthdays are especially difficult when the happy celebration of the surviving child may conflict with the sad emotions of the parents. Some parents find comfort in lighting an extra candle for the dead twin. Later, the surviving child may like to join in the ceremony. Other parents may choose to set aside a quiet period on anniversaries when they can think specially about their child who has died.

To many bereaved parents the sight of another couple with twins may provoke painful feelings of jealousy. This is particularly difficult for parents who had already made many friends at their local twins club. They can, however, be assured that many parents there will be longing to help even if they do not know how to. They want to be in touch, yet fear that their own good fortune may add distress. They will be only too delighted if the bereaved couple show they value their help or friendship.

Many bereaved parents find particular comfort in talking to others who have lost a twin. Several countries now have special bereavement support groups which provide a network of contacts as well as newsletters. We have also started a Bereavement Clinic in London on the same broad lines as the Special Needs Clinic described on p. 88.

12

The Single Surviving Twin

A SURVIVING TWIN will usually feel the loss of his twin brother or sister far more deeply than the loss of an ordinary sibling. Strangely enough, this may still be so even when they have never known each other—when one twin has died at birth or soon after.

The sense of loss and incompleteness felt by a surviving twin who has lost his twin at birth are illuminated in the Italian novel *I Fantasmi Della Mia Vita** by Achille Geremicca. As a child, the subject of the novel had longed for a companion to strengthen and comfort him; he had even created an imaginary twin. Later he discovered that he was in fact a single surviving twin—a "poor survivor, a sad remaining soul, a mutilated life, a mere half which, by itself, is as sad as a ruin."

There are many reliable accounts of this remarkably deep feeling of loss, even in people who did not know they were twins. Some have described how they felt lonely and strangely incomplete throughout their childhood. It is not uncommon for mothers to tell their surviving daughter about their twin when they are themselves thinking of having children. Several surviving twins have told me of the inexpressible sense of relief they felt when at last their childhood loneliness was explained.

Others are convinced that they were one of twins but fail to find tangible proof. One adult who believed she was a twin wrote, "For many years I felt that it was not me standing in my own body and I felt like I was someone looking on while my body did things." Perhaps she was a partner to a so-called "vanishing twin" (p. 5).

---

*Casa Editrice Alberto Stock, Rome, 1925.

. . .

Even though it may sometimes be painful to do, I believe that a child should always be told that he was a twin so that he can ask questions and express his feelings. He may at first be angry with his parents or with the hospital doctor who "allowed" his twin to die. There may be a sort of anger toward his twin for deserting him or for distressing the family. He may also feel guilt for having survived somehow at the expense of his twin.

Teachers at school or playgroup may be able to help children express their feelings through drawing or play. Indeed, so long as he or she has been told of the bereavement, the alert teacher may be able to give valuable help to a disturbed child.

Many twins and triplets are proud of their status. This was illustrated by a story in the *Lancet* in 1949. Two boys came for their school medical examination. When these indistinguishable children entered the examination room, the doctor asked cheerfully, "Twins?" "No," replied the boys in chorus. Deflated, the doctor consulted his notes which confirmed the same birth date. Having completed his examination, he irritably concluded, "You *are* twins." "No," came the reply "we are triplets." Their brother had died at birth.

Five-year-old Emma came to see me just to talk about Sophie, her stillborn twin. She was proud of being a twin and very interested in it. When I asked Emma if she missed Sophie she replied that she did but that she talked to her every day. "I know she can't talk but she likes to hear about what I am doing." Incidentally, these feelings were not instilled by any particular religious beliefs in the family.

A middle-aged head teacher of a primary school described a similar feeling of closeness to her twin sister who had died in infancy. "I often think and dream about my twin. Last year, during a bad attack of flu, I dreamed that I was so exhausted that my sister came and took over the running of the school. I didn't need to tell her anything. She knew it all instinctively."

In later childhood, death may be due to accident, chronic illness, or a sudden infection. Twins are no more likely to suffer and die from these than single children but when they do the impact on the survivor can be enormous. If the one who dies is the "leader" it can be devastating. The survivor can feel only "half a person" and the need therefore to absorb the dead twin's strength to carry on. Some African tribes actually say the spirit of the dead twin has to be preserved if the survivor is to remain whole. Such beliefs may be regarded as superstitions yet the symbolism can have a profound meaning to the surviving twin. A sophisticated Nigerian anthropologist from the Yoruba tribe who had lost her twin at birth told me she still treasured her twin's wooden image which traveled everywhere with her.

As I have said, many survivors feel guilty for being the one chosen to live. The survivor's guilt, of course, is the greater if he feels directly or even indirectly responsible for his twin's death. If the death resulted from, say, some prank they were involved in together, the survivor may need a lot of help in coping with his remorse, however irrational.

Younger children have a special difficulty in understanding the finality of death. They cannot believe their brother or sister will never return. Obviously, a child cannot be prepared for a sudden death, but if one twin has a long serious illness it is nearly always helpful if the other twin, however young, is involved as much as possible in the final stages of the illness, and at the death itself, as well as in the mourning. It is much better that he should cry and see others crying than bottle everything up. Moreover, for almost all of us the unknown and the unseen are far more bewildering and frightening than the reality. If the healthy twin is sent away to relatives or friends he will feel lonely and rejected, not only by his parents but also by his twin.

One 8-year-old boy whose twin brother died of leukemia after a two-year illness, gave enormous thought to choosing which precious treasures, including a pair of football boots, should be placed in the coffin. These symbols, rituals, and ceremonies are deeply meaningful to those involved and deserve our greatest respect.

While struggling to manage their own grief, many parents will find the sometimes disturbing behavior of the surviving twin especially distressing. He will often become withdrawn or destructive, perhaps for several months. But with bereavement counseling for the whole family and patience and understanding from their parents, such children almost always find themselves again and become able to talk normally about their dead twin.

Mythology provides many examples of the sense of desolation felt by the survivor at the loss of his twin. Castor and Pollux, the twin sons of Leda by Tyndareus and Zeus, had powers over the wind and waves and became known as the seafarers' guardians. When Castor was killed in battle, Pollux was so desolate that he begged his father, Zeus, to allow him to join his brother. They became the heavenly constellation Gemini, which means "twins."

According to one source, Narcissus, from whom the derogatory term "narcissism" or self-worship is derived, was also a twin, though a much maligned one. Narcissus had a twin sister to whom he was devoted and it was only after she had died that he spent long hours looking at his own reflection in a pool. On this interpretation his contemplation was not vanity, but a profound longing for his lost twin.

Through the work of Joan Woodward, a psychotherapist in Birmingham whose own identical twin sister died in early childhood, we have learned much about the profound and unique sense of loss felt by many adult single surviving twins. She interviewed over two hundred bereaved twins, more than one-third of whose twins had died within the first six months. In some cases she found that the loss was experienced equally deeply by those who had never consciously known their twin because she or he had died at birth or soon after. Some survivors whose twin had died early in life felt, whether justified or not, that their parents blamed them for the death of their twin. When this occurred the effect on the survivor was devastating.

Contrary to the commonly held assumption that feelings of grief lessen over time, some twins found that the pain continued for many years, sometimes increasing in intensity.

As a result of Joan Woodward's work, a group of thirty bereaved twins met in London in 1989. For the great majority it was the first time they had knowingly met another bereaved twin. Following this meeting and the widespread interest it created, a Lone Twin Network was established. This allows bereaved adult twins to be in touch with others who have lost a twin. There are twins on this register who have lost their twins at all ages from before birth to 84 years. Many have never before had the chance to share their experiences and the relief that some of them express about this is very moving.

Through the Network I have met a number of bereaved twins and many have shared their experiences with me in letters. Some whose twins had been stillborn wrote of their guilt and the feeling that their parents blamed them for the death. One said, "Because I was the bigger baby I was told I had taken my brother's food." Another, "I was untwinned at birth when my dear sister died having been starved (the doctor said) and finally kicked out by me." Some survivors felt their mother would have preferred the other twin to have survived, particularly if it was a different sex. To be the twin of a stillborn baby may be the worst fate of all. Many survivors appear to carry the onus for their twin's death right into adulthood.

John Hampson, a middle-aged man whose girl twin had been stillborn, described how, as a child, he had always divided his food into two and was reluctant to eat the second half. In his poem he tells of the guilt he felt:

> I didn't even say Goodbye
> Nine months together
> Sharing the warmth
> The beat of our mother's heart
> Her caring, her carrying
>
> Lighter than two bags of bread flour
> I lived
> But I hadn't shared, hadn't cared
> I didn't even say Goodbye
>
> Too late, I tried to share
> Divide my dinners
> Too late I tried to care
> Feed her. Feed her!

Was it caring? Sharing?
Instinct?
Guilt? Some infantile gesture of repentance?
Too late, those dreams of embrace
That closeness in the dark warmth

Oh, the guilt of all those years.

Later, he came to terms with his guilt in a service of healing.

Much is written about extraordinary coincidences of twins dying simultaneously even if they are miles away from each other at the time. A pair of identical 66-year-old twin men died on the same day from a heart attack. One was in Bristol and the other Windsor, ninety-three miles away. Identical 17-year-old boys, one celebrating the New Year in Glasgow and the other at sea with the navy, collapsed and died inexplicably within forty-eight hours of each other. These stories make news but they are, in fact, rare. A study in the United States of 1,400 elderly twins found that the average difference in the age of death was for identical men 4 years 2 months, for fraternal men 6 years 3 months, for identical women 9 years 6 months and for fraternal women 10 years 7 months.

The death of an adult twin leaves a surviving partner who must often endure an agonizing period of readjustment. No other bereavement threatens the identity of a person in the same way. Great as the tragedy of losing a spouse or a child is, at least the bereaved person is by definition an adult with a clear identity before he or she became a spouse or a parent. A twin is never anything but a twin and the loss of this most intimate and defining of relationships can undermine their basic sense of identity. Many people, in different ways, have echoed the twin who wrote that she felt "half of me is missing." Another twin wrote, "I find now that being alone is sometimes quite unbearable. The emptiness and grief that followed [the death of parents] was nothing like the awful hole that my life has now. I feel more alone than words can express. It's a strange feeling, I do not somehow feel a whole person any more."

Many twins have never even tried, or risked, imagining life

without their twin. One wrote, "Whenever I envisaged my old age it was always the two of us as little gray-haired old ladies— never as me alone." Another said, "My greatest problem is being one person after being part of two. My twin sister was the 'strong' twin. I was the willing follower."

Death by suicide calls forth especially agonizing and conflicting emotions. The twin may feel a deep sense of guilt that he had not been able to prevent the tragedy but also a deeper anger that his twin should have deserted him. Some identical twins might also fear that they, too, could have a propensity toward suicide.

Desertion can also be a strong emotion when a twin becomes addicted to alcohol or drugs. "How could he deceive me when we were so close?" is the question that so many twins of alcoholics ask. When one has shared every childhood secret it can be extremely painful to discover the deviously hidden bottles.

Whether identical twins in general feel the loss more than fraternal twins is not known, but the indications are that this is so. In Joan Woodward's study of bereaved twins, 45 percent of those who knew their zygosity were identical (compared to the expected 33 percent found in the general population). Of the first thirty-seven twins in the Minnesota Study of Twin Loss, twenty-five were identical and of those twins who have joined the British Lone Twin Network, 44 percent think they were identical twins.

For an identical twin the constant reminder in himself of his twin may be deeply painful. One young man, whose identical twin had died the year before, described the agony of his daily shave— "looking at my twin." Three years later it was still the most painful part of the day.

Early adulthood seems to be a particularly difficult time to lose a twin. Many such twins will not yet have embarked on independent lives. Some may be sharing careers. One identical twin in his early twenties had shared an art design studio with his brother. Although their styles differed, they were in harmony with each other and had sometimes done joint designs. More important, they had a constant source of companionship, understanding, stimulation, and encouragement. For this young man, as for many, his twin was not only his closest relative but also his best friend, and the bereavement doubly hard to bear.

For twins who have lived and worked together, the death of one can leave the survivor feeling so bereft as to doubt whether he will ever again function as a complete person. Norris McWhirter describes how after the sudden violent death of Ross, his twin, he felt he must make a definite decision. Either he was to become half a person and crumble or he must absorb the strengths of his brother and become a double person and continue with the work they had undertaken together. He resolved to do the latter and has successfully done so.

13

Higher Multiple Births

···

THEORETICALLY THERE IS no limit to the number of children that a human mother can carry in a pregnancy and many hoaxers and jokers in the past have taken advantage of this by telling exaggerated stories about multiple births. In 1951 Dr. Claudius Mayer reviewed all authenticated or legendary cases where the mother was said to have delivered six or more infants. He found a total of ninety-five such reports. Some, however, were undoubtedly duplicated cases which had been imaginatively embellished over the years.

The record in both number of alleged offspring and variations to the attributed number must be held by Margaretha, Countess of Hennenberg, who is variously described as having 350, 365, 366, and 1,514 infants in 1276. According to legend the Countess had scolded a beggar with twins for leading what she assumed must have been an immoral life if this had been the result. The beggar's response was to curse the lady that she should have "as many children as there are days in the year."

False allegations involving multiple births seem to have been a popular form of revenge. In 1872 an unrequited lover placed the following announcement in the local paper in Waren, Ohio:

On 21 August 1872, Mrs. Timothy Bradlee, Trumbull Co., Ohio, gave birth to eight children, three girls and five boys. She was married six years previously when on the day of her marriage she weighed 273 lbs.

It was not until 1914, after this story of octuplets had been reported in many national newspapers and medical journals, that a suspicious doctor investigated and discovered the hoax.

The largest number of fetuses that a mother has been reliably known to carry is nine, nonoplets. In at least one of the cases some of the babies were born alive but there are no confirmed long-term survivors. Octuplets, of whom seven are said to have survived, were allegedly born in 1947 in the village of Yang-Pang-Chen, 120 miles from Shanghai. The report, however, came from the father via an Italian newspaper and was never confirmed.

Several sets of septuplets have been delivered with some surviving children but the first complete set to survive was born in 1997. In England there are now three surviving sets of sextuplets, the six Walton girls, Hannah, Sarah, Kate, Lucy, Ruth and Jenny, who were born in 1983, the Coleman sextuplets, three boys and three girls, who were born in 1986, and a third set born in 1993. There are now a number of other surviving sets of sextuplets worldwide.

The majority of these very high multiple births now occur as a result of treatment for infertility either with drugs to stimulate ovulation or with the new techniques such as *in vitro* fertilization (IVF), when many embryos have been replaced in the womb. However, there have always been the occasional large multiple births from entirely natural causes. The most famous must be the Dionne quintuplets, identical girls, Marie, Emilie, Yvonne, Cecile, and Annette, who were born in a remote part of Canada in 1934 to a poor French-Canadian couple. The babies weighed a total of 11 pounds 1 ounce, with individual weights ranging from 1 pound 15 ounces to 2 pounds 14 ounces. They were delivered at home by their astonished doctor, Dr. Dafoe, who wrapped them in cotton wool and to everyone's amazement they all survived—an astonishing achievement at that time.

The Bushnell sextuplets, who were all born alive in Chicago in 1866, attracted surprisingly little publicity. Two died in infancy but the other four survived at least until their late sixties.

Although many large sets, including triplets, occur as a result of infertility treatment, there are many who do not and for some parents they may come as a complete shock, sometimes a most unwelcome one. Julia had three boys of 8, 6 and 4 but after much deliberation she decided to have a very last try for the much-wanted girl. Quads were diagnosed at fourteen weeks. Julia was horrified; her husband had been reluctant to have another child anyway, and four was unthinkable. Throughout the pregnancy Julia was extremely depressed and worried. We all prayed that it would not be four boys. At thirty-four weeks she had a quartet of healthy, bouncing babies all weighing over $4\frac{1}{2}$ pounds—two identical boys and, thankfully, two identical girls.

Higher multiple births, like twins, may be identical or fraternal or a combination; that is, with one pair or even two pairs, of identical within the set. Triplets which arise from three different eggs are trizygotic. Triplets arising from two eggs—only one of which has split—are dizygotic. Monozygotic triplets arise when one egg splits once and then one of the halves splits a second time.

Until recently the proportion of these three types of triplets amongst Caucasian populations was half trizygotic, one-third dizygotic, and one-sixth monozygotic, a ratio of 3:2:1. As we shall see later, however, these ratios have been altered by infertility treatment.

Quads and more are made up of similar combinations. Monozygotic quads can be "symmetrical," that is, if one egg splits and then both halves split again, or "asymmetrical" if one of the two halves splits and then one of them splits again. There is, of course, no way of telling the form or origin of a particular set.

Most of the sets born as a result of treatment for infertility will be fraternal as they arise either because of the increased number of eggs produced by the mother or because of the large number of embryos replaced (see p. 113). Occasionally, however, an identical pair will occur within a set. Mary had already had two unsuccessful attempts at IVF. For the third time, three embryos were transferred to the womb. Two weeks later she was overjoyed to discover she was pregnant. Four weeks later she was amazed to be told she was having quads, one of her embryos had divided into two.

One might expect this division to happen by chance about three or four times per thousand pregnancies as it does in "normal" pregnancies. It seems, however, that identical twins occur more often than this amongst women treated for infertility. Although so far unexplained, this discovery may provide clues to the cause or causes of identical twinning in general.

It was once thought to be relatively easy to calculate the incidence of triplets if the incidence of twins was known. A German scientist, Dr. Hellin, stated that if the frequency of twins in a certain population was one in X, then the frequency of triplets was one in X^2, and that of quads one in X^3, and so on. Thus if one in 100 pregnancies resulted in twins, one in 10,000 would produce triplets and one in 1,000,000 would produce quads. This rule, known as Hellin's Law, worked quite well until hormone treatment for infertility started to show its effects. Now the incidence of triplets is nearly three times that expected by Hellin's Law and the incidence of quads is far greater still. There have been 47 sets of quads in England and Wales in the first half of the 1990s whereas there were a total of 5 sets in the second half of the 1960s, that is, before drugs were used for treating infertility.

Until 1980 the number of sets of triplets born in the UK each year ranged between 70 and 100. There has since been a steady increase and in 1996 there were 299 sets of triplets, as well as 9 sets of quads. In other countries, the number of triplet sets has increased even more dramatically than in the UK. With the increasing number of couples receiving treatment by these new techniques it is likely that the figures will continue to rise. They will certainly do so until such time as gynecologists can gauge better which embryos are likely to survive. There will then no longer be a need to transfer several embryos to give a good chance of a single pregnancy.

In addition to the increase in the number of triplet births there is an even greater increase in the number of surviving triplet children. Many of the babies who are now growing up as healthy children would never have survived before the recent improvements in the intensive care of very small babies. In a set of triplets born at twenty-six weeks, that is fourteen weeks early, all three may now survive, whereas a few years ago they would have been automatically defined as a miscarriage and the possibility of survival would not even have been considered.

The causation of triplets (other than those which result from treatment for infertility), is assumed to be the same as for twins (see chapter 1). There have been a number of families reported where a set of triplets has followed a set of twins. The record appears to be held by an eighteenth-century Russian peasant (described on p. 8), whose family is said to have included 7 sets of triplets and 4 sets of quads. The current UK record is held by Mrs. Constable of Warwickshire who reportedly has 22 children, including two sets of twins and one of triplets.

Just as the ratio of boys to girls is somewhat lower in twins than in singletons, so it is with triplets. Indeed, the ratio is somewhat lower again, and there are slightly fewer triplet boys than girls.

As already mentioned, the number of higher-order birth children is increasing rapidly as a result of treatment for infertility. While many couples who badly want a child will be prepared to risk having triplets (occasionally more), in order to increase the chances of having one child, very few of them would choose to have such a number. Even those who are initially thrilled at the prospect of a ready-made family of three, often have little idea of the price they may have to pay. Not only are there extra risks to the babies' health because of prematurity and low birth weight but the physical, emotional, and financial stresses in caring for them may be enormous.

Sextuplets have been born and survived as a result of drug treatment for infertility. The first surviving IVF quads were born in Australia in 1984 and the first IVF quints in the UK in 1986.

Since the first so called "test-tube baby," Louise Brown, was born in 1978, the IVF technique has become widely accepted as a means of enabling an infertile couple to have a child. However, the success rate is still relatively low. In the 1995 Annual Report of the British Human Fertilization and Embryology Authority (HFEA), which is the body providing guidelines for the practice of IVF in the UK, the overall success rate for 1993 was calculated to be 14.2 live births for each hundred treatment cycles.

The success rates do vary greatly between the clinics involved. The larger and more experienced ones may achieve a live birth rate as high as 30 percent whereas some small, recently established units are yet to produce a live birth. Of the pregnancies achieved in 1993, 70.1 percent were singletons, 25.6 percent were twins, and 4.4 percent were triplets.

In the IVF procedure, the eggs which have been collected from the woman are placed with the sperm of her partner (or a "donor") in a culture dish. When the eggs have fertilized and divided into about four cells a number of these fertilized eggs, or pre-embryos, will be transferred into the mother's womb. The more that are transferred the greater are her chances of becoming pregnant. Figures for 1993 in the HFEA report show that the pregnancy rate if one pre-embryo was transferred was 8.7 percent, whereas for two it was 20.9 percent, 24.6 percent for three.

Not surprisingly, the risk of a multiple pregnancy (twins or more) also increases with more embryos. Only 2.5 percent of the induced pregnancies produced twins or more from the transfer of one embryo but 22.0 percent did so for the transfer of two and 33.2 percent for three. However, several units now find that if more than two good quality embryos are available for transfer, the woman's chance of becoming pregnant is just as good following the transfer of two embryos as of three.

Similar figures, which are still probably underestimates, are reported with gamete intrafallopian tube transfer (GIFT). With the GIFT technique, eggs and sperm are again mixed but then immediately transferred to the fallopian tubes leading into the womb so that fertilization can take place in the mother's body. A survey in Britain in 1989 showed that about two thirds of triplets were conceived following some form of treatment for infertility.

In 1997 there were seventy units in the UK who performed IVF and there is every indication that these numbers will continue to climb. This may be happy news for infertile couples but as the number of centers increases, will the number of higher-order births do likewise? It may well do so until research is successful in determining how the chances of a single embryo developing into a healthy baby can be increased. Couples will then be able to have the baby they long for without risking these high multiple pregnancies with all their attendant hazards.

Many advances in medicine pose ethical or moral dilemmas but few are more complex than those arising from the new technologies for the treatment of infertility. The dilemmas are increased by the involvement of at least three people—the mother, the real or potential baby (or babies), and the father. The following case will illustrate some of the complications.

A couple in their late thirties decided to seek help again with conception. Their only previous child, a 3-year-old daughter, had been conceived with the help of ovulation-stimulating drugs.

This time IVF was recommended. On the first attempt seven eggs were retrieved, six were successfully fertilized, and the obstetrician recommended transferring four of the embryos. The parents were told that their chances of having one child would be significantly increased by transferring so many embryos; there would be a small chance of having twins but the chances of quads were said to be too small to consider.

At five weeks, the ultrasound scan showed more than one developing embryo and, three weeks later, four fetuses were confirmed. After the initial shock, the parents' main concern was for the babies" survival, health and care. Could all the babies survive and be healthy? If so, how could they afford the huge extra costs? How could they carry, feed, and care for so many? How could they give each child the love and individual attention he or she deserved, let alone continue to give the elder child the attention she needed and had learned to expect. Yet quads would be exciting; how proud they would feel as parents. All these thoughts and more were jumbled in their minds as they began to look ahead.

The next day, however, their obstetrician confronted them with the suggestion that it might be best to reduce the number of fetuses by two (by killing the other two in the womb). This, he said, would give them a much better chance of ending up with healthy babies.

The parents were stunned. Neither of them had previously

heard of the procedure which is called fetal reduction, selective reduction, selective feticide, or selective birth, let alone thought about its many implications. The mother was horrified but the father, a scientist, was used to weighing balances of probability and decided the suggestion should be considered seriously.

The parents had always thought that their ideal family would be two children. They had asked for help in producing *one* child, not four. On the other hand, they did not want to sacrifice any precious baby which they had had such trouble in conceiving. Anyway, they thought, how does one choose to "keep this one and not that one?" What if one of the survivors was abnormal or just a difficult baby? How would one then feel about the potentially perfect child that had been sacrificed? And how would a surviving child feel about his parents' actions; might he himself feel guilt as a survivor? Finally, might the procedure itself damage one of the survivors or even cause the whole pregnancy to miscarry?

"Even if we do end up with two healthy children, how will we feel as parents about the ones who died? Can we cope with that guilt?" they asked. Unfortunately, there are very few knowledgeable people to talk to about these dilemmas. And suddenly this couple who only a few weeks before had been fervently hoping that they might be among the lucky 10 percent or so of IVF couples who manage to have *one* baby were now facing an apparently insoluble moral problem.

For each couple the balance of risk and advantage will be different but for all there will be tremendous anxiety, responsibility, and sometimes agony. Not surprisingly many couples disagree with each other as to the best plan. There can be no "right" solution, every response involves some risk and much pain. Yet a decision has to be made and soon.

Even couples who freely decide on selective reduction may well need long-term support. One or both of the parents may later feel much more grief than they expect at the time of their decision.

New infertility treatments have created other dilemmas. What, for example, should happen to the remaining embryos not selected for transfer? Should they be frozen and kept for possible future pregnancies? Is it of any importance to the parents or the children themselves if their conception and birth were long separated? Or that some of their children may be of different ages yet "conception twins?" If unwanted, should the embryos be discarded? Or should they be donated to someone else? May they be experimented upon and, if so, for how long?

A basic and very sensitive question is how many embryos should be transferred. Many, including the Human Fertilisation and Embryology Authority would say a maximum of three. Some would recommend only two, at least for the first attempt. In trying to sort out these dilemmas, there is the issue of who should decide: the parents, the doctors, the law, or all three?

I have not dealt with any of the legal implications; the law does not yet provide for many of the issues and what regulations there are vary between different countries. The dilemmas I have mentioned, and many others, will need to be kept under review both by givers and receivers of treatment and by ordinary people who are concerned for the welfare and the rights of their fellow citizens and their children. We should indeed all be involved in such discussions and before too many parents have gone through these stressful experiences.

The pregnancy of a mother carrying three or more babies is not necessarily different from any other kind of pregnancy except that she is likely to feel large and often uncomfortable much earlier on. However, the chances of complications such as high blood pressure and premature labor are higher and for these reasons most mothers will be admitted to the hospital at some stage for bed rest, and some may feel they have no choice but to spend much of their time in bed because of the discomfort of carrying such a load.

The length of pregnancy with triplets or more varies much more widely than with single babies but the great majority of triplets will be born prematurely, that is, before thirty-seven weeks. The average length for a triplet pregnancy is about thirty-four weeks and for quads thirty-two and a half weeks, compared with forty weeks for a single pregnancy and thirty-seven weeks for twins.

When it comes to the delivery, obstetricians seem to vary

greatly in their practice. Some will nearly always perform a caesarean section while others will prefer to deliver triplets by the
normal vaginal route, unless there are special indications for a
caesarean. The most common of these is the awkward presenta-
tion, usually breech, of one or more of the babies.

As discussed in chapter 3, the more babies that are sharing
one womb the smaller they are likely to be. This is partly because
the babies are more likely to be born early but also because the
human womb, during the last third of the pregnancy, cannot nour-
ish several babies as well as it would do one. However, during the
most important earlier part of the pregnancy the nourishment is
usually quite satisfactory which means that the extremely premature babies, that is those born more than ten weeks or so early,
should be at very little disadvantage compared with a single baby
of the same degree of prematurity.

All I have said about the care of newborn twins, discussed in
chapter 3, applies no less to triplets except, of course, that some of
the problems may be that much greater because of the extra baby
and because the children are likely to be smaller.

Having said that, some triplets will be extremely healthy,
bouncing babies and I have seen trios, where all weigh over 6
pounds, who go straight to the general ward with their mother.

14

Supertwins in the Family

···

LIFE WITH YOUNG TRIPLETS—and even more with quads, quints, and sextuplets—is in many ways an exaggerated version of life with twins, described in earlier chapters. The noise is greater, the pile of diapers higher, the number of bottles larger. Yet there are some differences great enough to deserve description and comment.

To take triplets, perhaps the most dramatic difference arises from the unfortunate fact that a mother has two arms and not three. I met one mother who managed to bottle-feed three babies simultaneously by holding a bottle in each hand and one between her knees. This ability and ingenuity is, however, exceptional and for most mothers the lack of a third hand is a distinct disadvantage. Many mothers of triplets are desperately frustrated by their inability to comfort three crying babies at the same time or to hold three hands to cross the road or, most significantly of all, to carry three babies at once.

Much of the information on the lives of families with triplets and more has recently become available through a series of linked surveys: the United Kingdom National Study of Triplets and Higher Order Births. This project was undertaken by the Office of Population, Censuses and Surveys, the National Perinatal Epidemiology Unit, and the Child Care and Development Group at Cambridge University. An attempt was made to collect information relating to higher-order births between 1979 and 1985 (with the exception of 1981, when there was a strike by those collecting birth statistics), although the survey of parents included births up to the end of 1988. The study covered medical and social aspects from the time of conception. One of the most important sections was concerned with the experiences of the families.

A major problem is the effect on other children in the family, illustrated by the unthinking exclusion of other brothers and sisters from photographs. An extreme example arose at the confirmation of a 13-year-old single boy attended by his whole family, including 10-year-old triplets. Afterward, the press photographer demanded a photograph of the bishop with the triplets. The mother naturally insisted that the confirmation candidate should be included. Some families have made it a strict rule that no press photographs may be taken unless siblings are included.

Being the brother or sister of triplets is a most unenviable position. Hard as the parents try to boost him or her, the sibling is often relegated to the background. Often their only claim to fame will be as "the brother (or sister) of the triplets." The triplets are not only demanding: they get by far the most attention from relatives, friends and passersby. A sibling who is considerably older than the triplets will at least have a responsible and somewhat unusual role to play, but life is especially hard for the toddler who is displaced by an attention-attracting trio. The needs of the sibling should be emphasized to friends and family alike so that he can be given compensatory attention.

Rosemary came to our Supertwins Clinic, not because she had any worries about her 6-month-old triplets but because she was deeply concerned about her 4-year-old daughter Louise. She and Louise had always had an exceptionally happy and close relationship before the babies were born. Rosemary had also prepared her daughter as best she possibly could for the arrival of the babies and emphasized how important her role would be. This proved all to no avail. Louise was bitterly jealous of her baby sisters. She was extremely rude and disobedient, especially to her mother from whom she refused all physical affection, rejecting any cuddles or kisses that were offered. Her behavior became more and more difficult and demanding; indeed, she became so aggressive toward the babies that she could not safely be left alone with them.

It was clear that Louise needed to have more time alone with her mother. But how could Rosemary achieve this without help?

The only regular assistance she had was someone to take Louise to and from school each day: just what was not, in fact, wanted. Instead it was arranged that this person should look after the babies while Rosemary herself took Louise to school. At least that guaranteed that there was some time in the day which was entirely Louise's and not interrupted by the dreaded trio.

If it is difficult to allow twins the range of opportunities that a single child would take for granted, it is a great deal harder with three or four children of the same age. For safety's sake triplets are often confined to a relatively small space. Only with reins for each of her 3-year-old quads would one mother take them for a walk in the park on her own.

As with twins, it is essential that each child should be thought of and treated as an individual. In that respect it is sometimes an advantage to be the "odd one out" either in sex or zygosity. The child who is easily recognizable has much more chance of being treated as a distinct being.

Nevertheless, although his individual identity is more assured, the "odd" child may lose out in his relationship with other members of the set. Identical pairs tend to gang up together. In one family, the red-haired, taller nonidentical girl was more confident and the leader until she was three. She then became increasingly aware of the powerful unit formed by her smaller fair-haired sisters. Not only did they attract a lot of attention but they often excluded her from their secrets, and so undermined her confidence.

Sometimes it is a mother's attitude that will isolate one child. In one set of quads the mother appeared never to have forgiven the first-born boy whose difficult delivery led to a caesarean section for the other three babies. To an outside observer this child appeared no more tiresome than the other three but the mother always referred to him as "the naughty one." Inevitably he started to live up to his reputation.

Esther Goshen Gottstein, in her study of some Israeli families, found the difficulty that mothers had in giving themselves to several infants at the same time was extreme. Those who had some previous experience, such as nursery teachers, were at a distinct advantage.

A strong mother with relatively "easy" twins may manage to cope satisfactorily on her own. A mother of triplets cannot and should not have to attempt looking after three babies at once. It is more than just exhausting: there are simply not enough hours in the day. A study by the Australian Multiple Births Association showed that it took $197^1/_2$ hours per week just to care for baby triplets and to do the household chores. The problem is that there are only 168 hours in a week.

In the National Study of Triplets, Dr. Frances Price repeatedly found that help for families had been completely inadequate and often slow to arrive. Too often the parents became ill and exhausted before help was provided. For many helpers, as well as parents, the practicalities of caring for so many babies was daunting. As Professor Marie Clay discovered in her review of the world literature on quads, very little information is available on the care of these supertwin families.

What is the best help? Obviously it will vary between families, not only depending on what is available but also on what the parents themselves choose to delegate and what they prefer to do themselves.

Clearly, fit grandparents living nearby with time to spare are invaluable but such are rarely available. Most families of triplets find themselves, at best, with occasional help from assorted family and friends. Many relatives can feel overwhelmed by the task; the amount of help they can realistically offer can seem so inadequate that they may opt out altogether. A number of grandparents have actually stopped visiting because they found the turmoil so daunting and some have even moved from the district!

For those who can afford one, a nanny will greatly help, especially if she is prepared to join the nighttime rota. But most people, of course, will not be able to afford this and, plainly, community and social service agencies should be more prepared to provide coordinated help. Unfortunately, present resources are so stretched that they will often only respond when a crisis threatens. Even when a crisis can be confidently predicted it is often hard to get the necessary help. Governments still sadly underestimate the value and cost-effectiveness of preventive medicine and social welfare.

One London mother, struggling alone during the day with a 4-year-old daughter and 6-month-old triplets, was told that no help was available but that if she really could not cope the babies could be taken into care. Terrified that her babies might be taken from her, the poor mother kept going somehow for another few weeks until she collapsed altogether. Some professionals fail to appreciate how hard it is for a mother to admit that she is not coping. When she does, her plight should be respected. One mother took a week to pluck up courage to tell her health visitor that she just could not cope any longer. The health visitor's only response was, "Well, you *are* coping, so don't worry." The mother felt her last hope of help had gone.

In another case, healthy quads spent an unnecessary extra week in the Special Care Baby Unit at great cost to the Health Service just because there was no one to help the mother at home with her four babies *and* her three older children.

Another mother, after six months of trying to cope with her four baby boys and a 3-year-old, reluctantly sent two of the babies to Kenya to live with her parents. When they returned a year later it was no surprise to find that they did not recognize their mother and displayed disturbed behavior for several months. The long-term financial costs of such episodes, let alone those of human happiness, could be very considerable.

Other sources of help have been discussed on p. 30. All of these are worth exploring for families with triplets, and it is vital to start early in the pregnancy: bureaucratic processes tend to move at a snail's pace.

As I have already said, parents differ about the assistance they find most useful. Some will want most help with the babies so that they themselves can have time with older children or escape from the house, even if only to do the shopping. Others will value help with the housework so that they can concentrate on the babies. Whatever form the help takes, it is bound to involve other people coming in and out of the house. For some mothers, indeed couples, this can be very trying. Those who value their privacy and have not been used to an "open door" way of life may find the intrusions extremely stressful.

Many mothers also find it hard to watch other people "mothering" their babies. They may feel possessive and long to give the same loving care to each that they would if he or she was an only child. One mother of quads told me of the jealousy she felt every time her nanny picked up a baby, especially when it was obviously comforted by this. She knew full well how highly irrational this was since there was no way she could hold all four of her babies at once.

The arguments for and against breast-feeding have been discussed in chapter 4. In the parents' survey of the National Study of Triplets, Dr. Frances Price found that just over half of the mothers gave their babies some breast milk. Some confined this to expressing milk while on the Special Care Unit. About 10 percent fed their babies for over two months. Most of those mothers developed a rota, either breast-feeding two and bottle-feeding one or vice versa. One mother fed her babies entirely on breast milk by expressing enough milk into a bottle between the feeds for the other two and I have known two other mothers who have entirely breast-fed their triplets. Mrs. Keys, whose quads were born in 1915, is said to have entirely breast-fed all four babies until they were 9 months old. One mother of quads chose to breast-feed one baby at each feed in order that she should have half an hour a day alone with each baby.

Transport of three or more babies is always a problem. Initially a large twin carriage will suffice and later many mothers will acquire a triple buggy or a double and single buggy which will clip together.

Many mothers find it quite impossible to get out alone with the children and therefore become very isolated. Visits to a doctor can be an ordeal and it is important that the health visitor should appreciate the extra needs of the family, not least the extra hands for carrying. Most families have to change to a larger car, usually a station wagon if not a minibus. Parking can be a problem if long walks with three or more children are to be avoided. One family with quads found they could always get special parking facilities at public events if they telephoned in advance.

Few people appreciate the enormously greater cost of a multiple birth family when compared to a large number of single children. Perhaps the worst aspect is that clothes and equipment cannot be handed down. Three high chairs, three cribs, three car seats, and so on, demand what for most families is a huge financial outlay, not to mention that of a larger car, or larger home. With a family that is only gradually adding to its numbers, there is less urgency, but with triplets everything is needed at once.

On top of all this, a working mother is likely to take much longer to get back to work and the father may be torn between earning much needed overtime money and hurrying home to help with the babies.

The sight of three babies in a stroller is enough to turn all heads in the street, so it is scarcely surprising that the media are greatly attracted to higher-order birth families. For some this media attention may just be amusing; for a few it may be profitable; for many, however, it may become very tiresome. One family reduced the size of the crowd that always gathered around their triplet carriage by attaching a large sign saying "Donations Welcome!" It is not only for financial reasons that the Waltons employ an agent: they also need someone to control the press which would no doubt have hounded them constantly over the first few years of the sextuplets' lives.

Perhaps the most publicized of all sets of supertwins were the identical Dionne quintuplets from Canada. In the 1930s a million-dollar enterprise was built up around the girls. A special arena was constructed in which the children would play as thousands of visitors trooped round the gallery to watch them as if at a zoo. Without the income this publicity generated their parents could never have afforded to feed and clothe their children but the sacrifice of privacy and of the quality of family life must at times have felt almost intolerable.

It is often assumed that families with supertwins must be rich from all the sponsorship they receive. The National Study of Triplets completely refuted that. It was found that although 75 percent of families with triplets received either national or local press coverage, few derived any financial benefit from it. A discount at the local shop or a few months' supply of milk or diapers was usually the most they got. A few families with quads or more sometimes benefited from selling rights to an exclusive feature to magazines but then often found the copy was pirated, and they themselves misquoted, in further articles generated from the original one.

One family found that only by insisting on payment did the volume of attention from the media remain at a manageable level.

Many parents of triplets have been distressed by the thoughtless or intrusive comments by friends or strangers. It appears that, quite unjustifiably, critical comments are much more likely to be directed at those whose babies result from infertility treatment, the implication being that they have "asked for it"—a particularly cruel accusation to a couple who may have been trying desperately for many years to have *one* child. No couple asks for triplets.

Despite all the difficulties and hazards, there is no doubt that most members of triplet and higher-order sets become healthy adults within the normal range of intelligence. There is every sign that this will be the case with the first British sextuplets: they are now doing well at primary school. However, there has so far been no large study that compares the overall development of supertwins with those of singletons. One study of the growth of supertwins showed that, although most were well within the normal range, they did tend to be slightly shorter and considerably lighter than their single siblings.

Inevitably a small proportion of triplets will be disabled as a result of their extreme prematurity—but the problems are essentially the same as we have discussed in chapter 10.

If parents of twins welcome the chance to meet each other, parents of triplets do so even more. Many such parents have never met a set of triplets before, let alone talked to a mother or father about the practicalities of life with three babies. In several countries there are now special supertwins groups. The ABC Club, for instance, is in touch with over one thousand families throughout the German-speaking countries.

At our Supertwins Clinic, families enjoy a lunch together where they not only share their experiences but hear from the volunteer parents (some of whose triplets are now adults), that life really does improve and indeed becomes great fun. Of equal value is the reassurance that anxious expectant parents can derive from seeing so many healthy and happy children.

Further Reading

BOOKS FOR PARENTS

Clegg, Averil, and Anne Woolett. *Twins: From Conception to Five Years*. New York: Ballantine, 1988.

Cooper, Carol. *Twins and Multiple Births: The Essential Parenting Guide from Pregnancy to Adulthood*. London: Vermilion, 1997.

Friedrich, Elizabeth, and Cherry Rowland. *The Parents' Guide to Raising Twins*. New York: St. Martin's Press, 1990.

Leigh, Gillian. *All About Twins: A Handbook for Parents*. New York: Routledge, Chapman & Hall, 1984.

Noble, Elizabeth. *Having Twins: A Parent's Guide to Pregnancy, Birth & Early Childhood*. Boston: Houghton Mifflin, 1980.

Rosen, Maxine B. *Being a Twin, Having a Twin*. New York: Lothrop, 1985.

Wright, Lawrence. *Twins: Genes, Environment and the Mystery of Identity*. London: Weidenfeld and Nicolson, 1997.

BOOKS FOR PROFESSIONALS
(Some are also suitable for parents who are seeking more technical information.)

Baldwin, Virginia. *The Pathology of Multiple Pregnancy*. New York: Springer Verlag, 1993.

Botting, Beverley, Alison MacFarlane, and Frances Price, eds. *Three, Four and More: A Study of Triplet and Higher Order Births* (Population Censuses & Surveys Office), HMSO (London), 1990.

Bryan, Elizabeth. *Twins and Higher Multiple Births: A Guide to Their Nature and Nurture*, Edward Arnold (Sevenoaks), 1992.

Keith, Louis, Emile Papiernik, Donald Keith, and Barbara Luke. *Multiple Pregnancy: Epidemiology, Gestation, and Perinatal Outcome*. Carnforth Parthenon, 1995.

Twins in School. La Trobe Twin Study and Australian Multiple Births Association Inc, 1991.

Ward, R. H., and M. Whittle. *Multiple Pregnancy*. London: RCOG Press, 1995.

Addresses of Multiple Birth Organizations

....

International Society for Twin Studies, c/o Jaakko Kaprio, Department of Public Health, PO Box 41 (Mannerheimintic 172), FIN-00014, University of Helsinki, Finland

AUSTRALIA
Australian Multiple Births Association, PO Box 105, Coogee, NSW 2034

BELGIUM
Association Francophone d'Entr'aide Pour Naissances Multiples, Avenue Hulet 17, 1332 Genval, Belgium

CANADA
Parents of Multiple Births Association, 4981 Hwy #7 East, Unit 12A, Suite 161, Markham, Ontario, Canada L3R 1N1

ETHIOPIA
Ethiopian Gemini Trust, PO Box 3547, Addis Ababa, Ethiopia

FRANCE
Association d'Entr'aide des Parents a Naissances Multiples, 8 Place Alfred Sisley, 95430 Auvers sur Oise, France

GERMANY
ABC Club, Strohweg 55, D-6100 Darmstadt, Germany

INDONESIA

Nakula-Sadewa Twin Foundation, Jl Teuku Cik Ditiro 32, Jakarta Pusat 10310, Indonesia

JAPAN

The Japanese Association of Twins' Mothers, 5-5-20 Minami Aoyama, Minatoku, Tokyo, Japan

THE NETHERLANDS

Nederlanse Vereniging Van/Tweeline, Johan V. Oldernbarneveltlaan 56,2582 NV'S Gravenhage, Netherlands
Nederlands Tweelingen Register, Vrije Universiteit, De Boelelaan 1111, 1081 HV Amsterdam, Netherlands

NEW ZEALAND

New Zealand Multiple Birth Association, PO Box 1258, Wellington, NZ

NIGERIA

World-Wide Twins and Multiple Births Association, 3 Tiamiyu Street, Off Ayonuga Street, Fadeyi Ikorodu Road, Lagos, Nigeria

NORWAY

Tvillingforeldreforeningen, Arbinsgt 7,0253 Oslo 2, Norway
Trilogi, Bjaalandsgaten 1, N-4016 Stavanger, Norway

SOUTH AFRICA

South African Multiple Births Association, PO Box 785070, Sandton 2146, South Africa

SWEDEN

The Swedish Twin Registry, Department of Epidemiology, Institute of Environmental Medicine, The Karolinska Institutet, Box 60208, S-10401 Stockholm, Sweden

Svenska Tvillingklubben, Hermelinsvagen 8, S-433 70 Partille, Sweden

UNITED KINGDOM

Multiple Births Foundation (MBF), Queen Charlotte's and Chelsea Hospital, Goldhawk Road, London W6 OXG

The Twins Clinics, c/o MBF (see above)

The Lone Twin Network, PO Box 5653, Birmingham B29 7J4

Twins and Multiple Births Association (TAMBA), 59 Sunnyside, Worksop, North Notts, SB1 7LN

TAMBA Supertwins Group, c/o TAMBA

TAMBA Bereavement Support Group, c/o TAMBA

TAMBA Special Needs Group, c/o TAMBA

TAMBA Single Parents Group, c/o TAMBA

TAMBA Twinline, c/o TAMBA

Maudsley Hospital Psychiatric Twin Register, Institute of Psychiatry, De Crespigny Park, Denmark Hill, London SE5 8AF

UNITED STATES

The Center for Study of Multiple Birth, Suite 464, 333 East Superior Street, Chicago, IL 60611

Minnesota Center for Twin and Adoption Research, Psychology Department, Elliott Hall, 75 East River Road, University of Minnesota, Minneapolis, MN 55455

National Organization of Mothers of Twins Clubs Inc, PO Box #23188, Albuquerque, New Mexico 87192-1188

Triplet Connection, PO Box 99571, Stockton, CA 94709

Twin Services, PO Box 10066, Berkeley, CA 94709

The Twins Foundation, PO Box 6043, Providence, RI 02940-6043

World Multiple Organization, 1120 Linden Drive, Aurora, IL 60506

Bereavement Group, Anchorage Parents of Twins and Multiples Club, PO Box 200–353, Anchorage, Alaska 99520

USSR

Twins Club, I Am Yu, 3 Harchenko St 3, Leningrad 194100, USSR

Glossary

· ·

Alphafetoprotein
  protein produced by the fetus

Amnion
  inner lining of sac containing the developing fetus

Autonomous speech
  see Cryptophasia

Binovular
  see Dizygotic

Chorion
  outer lining of sac containing the fetus

Conjoined twins
  identical twins where separation is incomplete so their bodies
  are joined together at some point

Cryptophasia
  secret language of twins

Dichorionic twins
  two babies who have developed in separate chorionic sacs

Dizygotic
  formed from two separate zygotes

Dizygous
dizygotic

Embryo
developing baby during the first eight weeks of pregnancy

Fetofetal transfusion syndrome
condition in which blood from one identical twin fetus trans-fuses into the other via blood vessels in the placenta

Fetus
unborn baby from eight weeks of pregnancy until birth

Fraternal twins
see Dizygotic

GIFT
Gamete Intrafallopian Transfer—method of assisted concep-tion

Higher order birth
triplets or more

Identical twins
see Monozygotic

IVF
in vitro fertilization and embryo transfer—method of assisted conception

Monoamniotic twins
two babies who have developed in the same amniotic sac

Monochorionic twins
two babies who have developed in the same chorionic sac but not necessarily the same amniotic sac

Monozygotic
formed from one zygote

Monozygous
Monozygotic

Neonatal
first four weeks of life

Nonoplets
nine offspring from the same pregnancy

Octuplets
eight offspring from the same pregnancy

Prematurity
delivery before thirty-seven completed weeks of pregnancy

Preterm
see Prematurity

Quadruplets
four offspring from the same pregnancy

Quintuplets
five offspring from the same pregnancy

Septuplets
seven offspring from the same pregnancy

Sextuplets
six offspring from the same pregnancy

Siamese twins
see Conjoined twins

Stillbirth

delivery of a dead baby

Superfecundation

conception of twins as a result of two acts of sexual intercourse in the same menstrual cycle

Superfetation

conception of twins as a result of two acts of sexual intercourse in different menstrual cycles

Supertwins

triplets or higher-order births

Triplets

three offspring from the same pregnancy

Trizygotic

formed from three separate zygotes

Twin transfusion syndrome

see Fetofetal transfusion syndrome

Uniovular

see Monozygotic

Zygosity

describing the genetic makeup of children from a multiple birth

Zygote

fertilized ovum

index

∙∙∙